Love,
Hannah & Brian
XXX

MORE DORSET DIARIES

For my sons, my step-daughters, and their children.

"Noticing is, surely, the prime artistic activity" – *Charles Moore.*

MORE DORSET DIARIES
or *Life after Perdita*

DAVID EDELSTEN

With illustrations by
Helen Mitchell & Becky Unwin

HALSGROVE

First published in 2005 by Halsgrove
Text © 2005 David Edelsten

ISBN 1 84114 482 7

British Library Cataloguing-in-Publication-Data
A CIP data record for this book is available from the British Library

HALSGROVE
Halsgrove House
Lower Moor Way
Tiverton EX16 6SS
Tel: 01884 243242
Fax: 01884 243325
E-mail: sales@halsgrove.com
Website: www.halsgrove.com

Printed and bound in Great Britain by
The Cromwell Press, Trowbridge

FOREWORD

David Edelsten was my first cavalry commanding officer. I had been sent to his regiment to help them train for a tour of duty in Northern Ireland – 'dismounted', as the cavalry appropriately enough referred to infantry work. I was at once struck by his singular style of command – apparently rather distant, certainly thoughtful, invariably restrained, even understated, yet with an ability to go 'hands-on' at the *moment juste*, whether operational or recreational. I was equally struck by what and how he wrote. There was not, perhaps, a great deal of opportunity for literary creativity in the British Army of the Rhine in those days, but even so David Edelsten's writing stood out. I recall reading his training directive. It was all clarity, directness and the elegant phrase. How apt, I remember thinking, that a cavalry commanding officer should write "I want a handy regiment". It seemed to me the perfect metaphor: the handy hunter, the handy polo pony – the handy regiment. There was too a wonderful, authoritative economy in his instructions, such as: "shaving precedes breakfast". And I was much taken by his reminder that, whatever the circumstances, the normal courtesies must apply: "visitors to headquarters are to be offered hospitality appropriate to the time of day".

At the end of my attachment I asked to transfer to this rather special regiment, and I am glad to say that, I having taken with me for those six months a fine hunter, the regiment said 'yes'. In no small measure, therefore, the creation of the character of Matthew Hervey, the hero of my series of cavalry tales, is thanks to David Edelsten.

Like David, I was an army officer for thirty-five or so years. 'Formation' – how a man's character and ways are formed – is therefore of abiding interest to me. The author of these *Dorset Diaries* was undoubtedly formed in great part by Sandhurst and by his (our) regiment, the 13th/18th Royal Hussars (Queen Mary's Own) – now, following amalgamation, known as The Light Dragoons. But the foundations, I believe, go much deeper. We know from the diaries themselves that David is steeped in the lore of the English (specifically the Dorset) countryside, and this from birth. The rhythms and cadences, the habits and customs of Wessex are undoubtedly in his blood. It is thoroughly appropriate that Thomas Hardy is a commonplace of his thinking, just as it is also appropriate that Surtees should loom large in the thoughts of so experienced a horseman. There is Johnson too, and Sterne and Fielding and so many others, because David Edelsten is thoroughly primed in the great canon of English literature, which, as one Oxford professor remarked to me recently, is a heritage now denied his undergraduates except those from a handful of schools. And then woven into this literary tapestry is the magnificent language of Cranmer, Coverdale and the Jacobean and Caroline divines: the Book of Common Prayer, and the King James Bible – the 'Authorized Version'. This should not be surprising in an Old Cliftonian of the golden period, but it is a delight nonetheless.

And then there is Jane Austen. Jane's elegant, restrained prose, as well as her keen observation of manners in the country gentry, clearly inspires much of David's writing. We know, because he has told us in his diaries, that like Mr Knightley he does not consider himself to be 'a dressy man'. Are there other characters with which the diarist identifies himself? It is an intriguing thought, but a foreword is not the place to do more than set the hare running, so to speak.

Are these diaries elegiac? Do they celebrate – mourn, even – a lost and better world, an English pastoral overlaid with both Romanticism and the robust yet humane outlook of the Tory gentry? Perhaps. And perhaps they should too, for this is an Englishness that has seen the Nation through many trials – and probably will again. The pleasure of reading David Edelsten is often, however, his wryness, the metaphorical twinkle in the eye. He may tilt at many things, and he can certainly rail, but his writing is, for the most part, gentle, shrewd, even oblique, leaving the reader with a deal of thinking for himself to do.

David Edelsten's *Dorset Diaries* could be subtitled *Far from the madding crowd*. Here is that same economic style and apt choice of phrase which struck me so forcefully in Germany over thirty years ago, a voice at once recognizable and distinctive. It connects today's frequently bewildering and exasperating world with, again in the words of Thomas Gray's *Elegy in a Country Churchyard*, 'The rude Forefathers of the hamlet'.

In truth, I know no-one who is writing of life in the English countryside with so fine a voice.

Allan Mallinson

INTRODUCTION

IN offering a sequel I am wary of disappointing those who have been so kind as to enjoy *Dorset Diaries*, but I found that a sequel had to be written. When I sought permission to put some of my *Country Life* pieces together in the earlier book, the Editor took the opportunity of discontinuing the page. I cannot at all blame him, I had had a good run: magazine publishing is a cut-throat business which no-one understands better than an editor.

He delivered the *coup de grace* as kindly as such a thing could be done, but I was left, as it were, an amputee hobbling on one leg, the missing one still strongly twitching. I had not realized how much I had come to depend upon writing about what I saw around me, and so could not, and did not stop noticing and, as I call it, doing words in my head.

The two opening sections, which I have called Spring and Summer, comprise observations, mostly from this house, this village, and the small patch of Dorset that is within riding distance. Written more-or-less in 'real time' as they say, it is in effect a diary, rather a selective one, of the first half of the past year.

Looking forward is not always a favourite occupation when one gets to a certain age, and in the section called Autumn I have chosen to reverse the crass Blairite slogan of last May's General Election and look back. In a haphazard sort of way it is autobiographical. I have written about things that seem to have mattered to me, returning again and again to this house, which matters probably more than it ought.

I should warn those who do not approve of it that the final quarter of the book is devoted to hunting: at the same time I beg them, if they have been so kindly patient as to have read that far, to read on. I am a great believer in the two factions trying to understand and to respect each other: we are, after all, all human, and, within the circle of those who are likely to read this book, probably trying to lead more-or-less virtuous and useful lives.

D.E.
The Old Rectory,
Glanvilles Wootton
Autumn, 2005

SPRING

"WHEN are you going to get another dog?" we are for ever being asked by friends who remember Perdita. We temporise, feeling slightly guilty; "Not immediately" we say. It is not just that Perdie is unforgettable, the dog of a lifetime, and irreplaceable; but, since part of the family has moved to Italy, where we visit frequently, it is a treat not to have to leave a miserable, betrayed and accusing dog behind. I suppose that "One day!" is the answer that we ought to give to those kind questioners; or "Some when!", as people round here still say.

Perdie haunts the house and garden, not a corner of which does not retain a memory of her twelve fairytale years with us. There is a wraith of her always in the kitchen, under the china-cupboard, where her beanbag used to be, and, in my mind's eye, she often jumps the gate ahead of me as I go out to visit the horses in our five-acre meadow. But hers is a gentle ghost, a reminder of a puppy rescued from destitution that lived with us 'happily ever after'.

Her leaving us has not been all loss. I could do without the rabbits, which get cheekier by the day, and have forced me to wire off the kitchen garden. Only this morning there were two of them to be seen playing in the stable yard when I drew the bathroom curtains first thing – I have never seen a rabbit there before.

And when we returned from riding mid-morning one was sitting bold as you please in the grass verge by the drive, not bothering to budge. It was only when Diana said "Myxomatosis?" that it took fright and hopped off, showing itself to be in perfect health. One day I am going to have to do something about the rabbits.

But the two old cats that have colonised our few acres, now they dare to, are animals of great character – independent, Rudyard Kipling cats. I smile when I see them, though they seem to have nothing whatever to say to me.

Only the other day the piebald tom, Sooty, was looking defiantly at me from under the water butt as I turned into the back yard. He of the adventurous spirit, who has been run over on the road, survived a broken jaw, more than once been given up for lost or dead, and has used up several of his nine lives, belongs to a neighbour with a small garden.

I do not in the least resent his trespassing, but I wish he would not walk over my car leaving muddy spoor from end to end. I can't imagine why he does it, it must surely be easier to walk round, or indeed under, but it prompts Diana to say that I ought to wash the car: I tell her she ought to have married an Air Commodore. (Forgive me if you don't get it. It's an old, very old and silly inter-service joke that would have it that RAF officers enjoy washing their cars when "a chap ought to be pig-stickin' or playin' polo. What!").

And the ginger tom, the gamekeeper's cat, is here there and everywhere on our land these days, hunting, or taking his ease; sometimes he sits on the top of a fence-post, like a carved pew-end – Perdie would have been after him like a bolt from a bow.

But it has to be said that we didn't have a sign of a rat in the stables this last winter – Perdie was completely baffled by their escape route, the ladder to the hayloft – no rats is at least something to be grateful for.

THE pheasants that have also moved in are positively welcome: in fact they are a daily joy. I love to see them strutting and clucking and showing off about the place. It has been a first chance really to study them, since I am a total twerp with a gun and don't shoot.

Their roosting habits have been a source of amusement and wonder through the recent winter. At the first sign of dark, as early sometimes as 3pm., they would start flying up into the trees, announcing to the world with wild squawks exactly what they were doing and where, as it were saying to any prowling foxes "Come and get me if you can!".

And now, in spring, their pairing and courting are a delight to watch. The cock birds, suddenly fearless, patrol the borders of their territory. One magnificent melanic specimen has established his rule in Chantry Mead, our five-acre field, where he finds splendid pickings under the hayrack, and beneath the feed-buckets on the gate.

Mr Black's territory – it's a name that does less than justice to the splendid variety of the dark glistening hues all about his plumage – evidently also stretches across the lane into our home paddock, where some invisible line separates it from that of Mr Brown, an Old English, or as a soldier might say, standard issue pheasant – he's not brown at all of course, he has gorgeous colouring, and a clerical collar, but his wife is distinctly drab.

Twice I have seen the two cock birds beak-to-beak, oblivious of all else, becking and bowing, the parson and the undertaker, as if in some stately dance, making strange rattling clucks and occasionally rushing at each other. I could walk almost within touching distance before they notice me, take alarm and make off. And that's another thing; I love to see a pheasant's clownish run.

At lunchtime today Mr Black was to be seen on the gravel drive outside the kitchen window, apparently fast asleep, ostrich-like, with his head stuck under a holly bush. He was there, taking his siesta, for the best part of two hours. I hope he knows what he is doing, and can cope with a surprise attack by a large tom cat.

I RECENTLY did two things that I had vowed never ever to do again... and on consecutive nights – spoke at a hunt dinner, and attended a hunt ball.

It was one wet February afternoon when I was watching Diana watch racing on TV, that a knock had come at the door. "I'm Andrew, not Simon" said our caller helpfully; his twin bother had been the last subaltern to join my regiment before I quit it some thirty years and more ago.

He didn't actually need to prompt me, they are alike as two foxhounds – ie not really alike at all if you understand what you are looking at. Like his brother, a lieutenant colonel now, he is chairman of the local pack of beagles, which, like his brother he had himself once hunted, and they were just then tow-rowing around the outskirts of the village, although you could barely hear them for the gale.

He had been let down by the speaker engaged for their Hunt Dinner, would I take her place? "Don't do it!" Diana pleaded, knowing what a tizz speaking engagements put me into, and how many sleepless nights might lie ahead. But he was clearly desperate, and it was difficult to say "No!". So I weakly agreed, and paid the usual price in loss of time and peace of mind: I had rather write a dozen articles than one speech.

In the event it passed off reasonably well – at least, people were kind enough to say so – but I shall not allow myself to get caught out like that again, I hope.

THAT WAS one of those mad weekends when events which one would much rather enjoy singly, elbow each other into the same crowded corner of the diary. For, on the next morning, we had our hunt scurry – an informal steeplechase – an innovation, and a great success. In the queue for the barbeque afterwards I met the Horse Whisperer who had wrought such a miracle persuading Bella, our tricky mare, that the Rice trailer was not a horse-trap a couple of years ago when we gave up the lorry.

The Horse Whisperer is rather a star in my world – I must tell you about her and what she does some other time – and I bumped into her again that evening at the hunt ball, when I went to get Diana's whisky, the only tipple my abstemious wife will drink. Along with several other hunt volunteers, Maya was serving behind the bar.

As with the beagle dinner, I had been outflanked over the hunt ball. Some-how it got into the diary, the tickets already paid for, before I had had any say in the matter. Seven years ago the occasion had been so much more of a brawl than a ball that I vowed never to go to another. But the word was that it would be much better this year; the venue was certainly promising, the Manor House in a neighbouring village.

Getting dressed for it after such an interval proved to be unsettlingly dramatic. I knew where my tailcoat was, and most of the necessary bits and pieces that go with it, but could I find a starched shirt? I searched everywhere, every drawer, every trunk, when, just as I was getting desperate and thinking of where I might borrow one, and who amongst my neighbours had a 15½ inch neck, something must have tripped my memory.

There were three shirts on wire hangers, ghostly in polythene shrouds, just as they had come back from the garage, in my wardrobe hanging ever so logically next to the tailcoat. (Our nearest garage, half-a-dozen miles away at Kings Stag, which never seems to close and where nothing ever is too difficult, is of course where one gets laundry done – where else?)

Dinner was actually at the ball, a great improvement since one did not have to wrench oneself away from a neighbour's friendly table and drive endless reluctant miles long after bedtime: and the 'music' was out of earshot. One way and another it was a great evening; no doubt we will go again.

IT'S betwixt and between times normally with the horses at this time of year: they are not completely 'in', and not yet fully 'out': not still regularly housed by night in the stable, nor yet quite turned away to grass.

But this year is an exception. Dandy did his best to kill me, by sitting on me, some weeks before Christmas, and I was kept out of the saddle for some time, so the two horses have spent the whole of this last mild, comparatively dry, winter in our meadow, with its hospitable, wind-defying shed. Dandy is partly clipped and in a rug, his sister Bella, who is a tough little thing despite her fancy ways, keeps herself snug in her own thick warm coat.

I call her 'little', in fact they are both well over sixteen hands high, but we have had them since they were foaled, and, just as our children never grow up in the mind's eye, our horses are like babies to me. I only hope that I may never be so foolish as to describe to you the sort of language that I habitually use when I am talking to them.

Dandy is now fourteen, his sister one year younger: their mother was a much loved Irish mare that we bought back from the Army in Germany where she was not enjoying saddle-club life, their father a gentleman lately resident in the stud round the corner in this village. We backed them and broke them in ourselves.

Although full siblings, and in many ways alike, they are quite unalike in looks and in nature. Dandy, a bay, is, to look at, the clone of his mother, though a slightly better horse, a typical crossbred hunter of a good type. Bella takes after her dad, might almost be mistaken for a thoroughbred, and has all the cranky ways, and more, that one expects in a highbred chestnut mare. Her mistress burst into tears when I told her that spring morning thirteen years ago that we had a newborn chestnut filly in our stable.

THERE was a light frost on the lawn this morning, and, as I walked down the drive to take yesterday's newspaper to my neighbour, I was looking anxiously to see how serious an event it had been. The tarmac was strewn with fragments that something, a squirrel I suppose, had chomped out of the chestnut trees during the previous night – a thing I have never noticed previously.

The flowering ends of twigs had been bitten straight through, each hand-sized fragment consisting of a grape-like cluster of tight buds, and three or four young leaves. I suppose that the growing twig, before it turns into wood, is succulent – the horses certainly seem to find them so, they graze mercilessly off them – a day or so later I noticed Bella hoovering up such of the fragments that had fallen inside the paddock railings.

Going out next, to bring the horses into the stable for a light breakfast before their morning work-out, I almost expected to find a skin of ice on their water trough, but there wasn't one. And, significantly, for the first time this year, they ignored the snick of the gate, didn't even lift their heads, let alone walk towards me to be caught, just went on stuffing themselves with the new young grass at the far end of the meadow.

These are the clues that one watches for very carefully in managing their diet as the seasons change, it is so vital to horses' welfare not to over-feed them. Already we have stopped their nuts, soon I shall have run their *Horsehage* down to nothing, and it will just be a question of when Dandy can do without his rug. Their winter coats are already coming out in handfuls – it's about the only time of the year that I really enjoy grooming them, it is so satisfying, and you feel they like it.

I had tried hard to listen to the weather forecast that morning. I always do, consciously, but invariably it has the same hypnotic effect; inevitably it seems my mind wanders off wool-gathering, just when they get to the crucial bit. What I did collect that morning was that the blackthorn winter – they don't call it that of course, one does not expect countryman's language on the BBC – was coming in the following week-end.

It will be quite soon enough to remove Dandy's rug by night when we finally turn off the central heating in the house, and Diana says "I don't think you really need bother with a fire this evening".

I AM always a little sad when, as this year, we get through to the spring without having gone skiing. It's a sport that I came to quite late in life, and got badly bitten by. I'm no good at it, but I can get down most pistes in my own inelegant fashion and in my own time. To me the great joy of it is to be able to spot your chalet or hotel from high up the mountain, and to know that you can get down to it, more or less in a twinkling, unaided. It's the nearest thing to flying.

Skiing of course clashes with other winter sports, and it is sometimes quite difficult to juggle conflicting priorities. But in the year of foot and mouth, with hunting and even marching for hunting stopped, *Country Life* sent me to write about Megève, the luxurious resort in the French Alps. It was the sort of plum that very occasionally emerges from the journalistic pie.

For a full week that March I was courted, best of all guided, overfed, massaged even, and generally spoiled: except that I was there wifeless, it was the best skiing I have ever known. Of descending the mountain on the last afternoon I later wrote, "For one reason or another I seem to shut my eyes a lot when skiing, especially on the 'black' runs. If you shut your eyes on the *piste* at Verbier or Val d'Isere, the sounds that assault your ears suggest Weymouth sands in summer: on that last run, of maybe half an hour, not one single skier shared the slope with me, and I skied in silence".

Megève, known at one time as the 21st Arrondissement because of its patronage by smart and wealthy Parisians, and, in the 1950s, Jean Cocteau and his set, is indeed exclusive, and well beyond my purse. If it afforded me my best skiing ever, my happiest skiing was one short precious time, long ago now, in crowded, chatty, friendly Verbier, when we had all four children with us.

"I THINK you're mad!"; "I enjoy being a little mad occasionally"; "Oh well – go on if you really think you want to". This was pillow talk; at breakfast it was "You'll have to dry him before you put his rug back on"; and later, when the full foolishness of my plans emerged, "You'll be going on that busy road, do you want to wear my yellow arm-band?"; "No thanks!" I said, and off I set towards the stable.

Unless there is a compelling reason not to, I ride one or other of our horses every day that God sends – I find that riding and writing go well together, the gentle pacing of a horse is conducive to sorting out ideas and stringing words together – sometimes Diana comes too, then we get both horses out. This particular morning had however set me a problem. Overnight a late equinoctial gale had come roaring in – outside it was as wild, and wet, and horrible as could be.

But I had previously determined to ride up to a small farm below the ridgeway at Dogbury where they sell game, to wheedle a Fête Draw prize out of the owner. It was to be the first longish ride I had done since Christmas, a fitness test prior to a promised half-day with the staghounds the following week. And, anyway, no doubt it is a grievous fault but I am not apt to alter plans previously made: I don't like to be driven off course, least of all by a spot of rain.

Unlike on the previous day, the horses were glad enough to come in. They both started to stride towards me from the far end of the field as soon as they saw me, pausing only to ease themselves in various ways – I was grateful to them for not saving it up for the stable. They came in quietly enough – I was grateful for that too – usually a gale makes them silly, and a mite dangerous if you are not nimble, as I am not at present.

There was a poplar branch down in the paddock, and, as I later learnt, the wind had bowled over our Christmas tree in the back yard, shattering its pot – the *coup de grâce* we reckon, it has not been looking at all well or happy since its last spell of duty indoors. What other casualties would we discover I wondered, no doubt the odd slate off the roof?

Soon Dandy was saddled up, Bella shut in her box – she would go mad without her brother if I were to leave her out in the paddock – and we set off into the rain, the wind mercifully dropping.

THE best rides by my reckoning are those when you do not have to retrace a single step, and when you have a particular purpose, an errand of some sort to run, it might be collecting eggs from the poultry farm, delivering a message, or returning a borrowed book. I like to do business on horseback, just like my father would from choice, his stethoscope in his jacket pocket, combine visiting patients with getting the horses out.

As we left the village I had a circular ride mapped out in my head which would take us up onto the ridgeway and last the best part of two hours. Needing to get a move on we trotted down the drive, Bella's operatic laments getting rapidly fainter, out of the village, past the "Fight Prejudice…" sign on our old giant ash, all the way, about a mile, to the egg farm, where a great house, Middlemarsh Grange, once stood. Then we cantered the short strip of old common in front of it – by which time we were both glad enough to walk and catch our breath.

Kennels Lane, our route west out of the village, which for half of its length is accompanied by a deeply embanked winding stream, is a place of great beauty, marred only by the rubbish that feckless people will strew there.

On this morning it was a month since I had cleared it of litter, and I made a mental note to return. My step-grandson, Jasper, soon to be seven years old, was shortly due to stay with us. He would enjoy helping me. Even if no other child in the whole kingdom, seemingly, is taught to pick up litter, I am determined that Jasper shall be.

Soon, the rain just a scatter now and the wind dropping, we hit the old Sherborne-Dorchester turnpike, the 'top road' as we call it, busy and sadly unrideable these days, crossed it, and, making the bar of an 'A' as it were, joined the less lethal road to Cerne Abbas that forks away from it close by.

I HAVE very strong views about riding on roads, and they bear on the behaviour of the rider. He must, I hold, make every effort not to impede traffic, and be seen by drivers to do so; always getting off the road, onto a verge, or into a handy gateway if there is one; always trotting smartly on if there is a blind corner or a crest ahead – if the occasion serves, ignoring what we learnt in the Pony Club about not doing so on tarmac, I often canter; always signalling as helpfully as possible when it is safe to over-take.

Above all the rider must semaphore and smile his gratitude to drivers who pass carefully, he may do this ironically to those very few who don't, but drivers must **see** his thanks, however preoccupied he may be in managing his mount. I can't count the number of times I have been told by someone of passing a rider on the road who didn't even smile thanks. One is so apt to be thought rude and condescending when on a horse, on one's *high horse* indeed, that it is essential to allow for this, even to over-compensate.

Another thing that I feel very strongly about is responding to greetings: perhaps I have spent too long in a profession where such courtesy is routine, salutes always answered. Along with answering letters, now-a-days replying to e-mails, and returning telephone calls, it is, as I see it, part of what we owe to the world, an essential part of good manners and of the social contract: only in those uncivilized places, large towns, do people habitually ignore each other.

The great majority of those who pass us in the road return my wave, but there is one particular type of driver that, gripping the wheel with both hands, stares rigidly to the front, beard bristling, spectacles a-glint. I wouldn't dream of confessing it, but, privately, I call them 'Guardian readers'. As they speed away I find it comforting to think that the foot on the accelerator pedal most probably wears that badge of the indoor office person, a sandal.

If you are wondering why I declined wearing the offered yellow armband, feeling as strongly as I do about considerate behaviour by riders using roads, I cannot give you a satisfactory answer. It is just that I refuse to go out riding on my 'native heath' looking like a Christmas tree. All proper people have a bit of the Knight of La Mancha in their make-up, which is no doubt why *Don Quixote*, 400 years old this month, is such a deathless book.

And if you are thinking that I have got it in for beards, you are wrong. Only the other day Bradfords, the builders' merchant's lorry passed me. I climbed Dandy up onto the high roadside bank amongst the knee-high nettles, dog mercury and wild garlic, so that it need not stop, but the driver halted beside us for a chat.

It was he who delivered the skelpings for our shed floor a couple of years back, and was so skilful managing his heavy lorry on the soft ground, and in the confined space available, that he dropped the load exactly where I had wanted it, and saved me hours of work. We chatted then, and hit it off.

For better or worse, an army life teaches one to make snap judgements about people, assess their TCQ, as I call it, their 'tight corner quotient'. He rates ten out of ten, although he has a beard.

WE ARE in 'Woodlanders' country now, in fact we are at the very spot where that loveliest of all Thomas Hardy's books begins, on "the forsaken coach-road running... from Bristol to the south shore of England... in the vicinity of some extensive woods". The vastness of Grange Woods is indeed on our right, Lyon's Gate ahead, and, a strange contrast on our left, a recently well-laid thorn hedge marks the edge of a hideous car dump. We press on.

Our business at the farm satisfactorily completed, Dandy faces the last steep climb to Dogbury Gate, where there was once a toll house. A thrush strikes up in the undergrowth as we turn east on to the ridgeway track, at last shaking off the traffic. Every time I ride that busy road I promise myself not to do so again, but the traffic this time had not been too heavy.

Hardy called this saddle in the escarpment of the Dorset Heights the Devil's Kitchen, because, seen from above, it is sometimes full of swirling mist, like a caudron. It features in *Tess of the D'Urbervilles*, and we are actually on the route that poor Tess followed that fateful winter's morning when she walked from 'Flintcomb-ash' (Plush), to 'Emminster', (Beaminster) to try to make contact with her defaulting husband's parents.

As we climb the wind strengthens, it's wild again, and again coming on wet. We are glad enough to leave the ridgeway track, the 'oldest road in Europe' some say, and follow the bridleway under the north shoulder of the summit, in the lee of Mount Sylva's iron age ramparts, and enter the shelter of a hanging wood.

The bridleway diverges from the main track through the wood. A notice marks the way ahead as 'Private': a massive pollard oak, clearly an ancient waymark on the public right-of-way gives the same message, but rather more politely. We quit the wood. Some distant cousin of Mr Black's explodes like a small landmine under Dandy's feet, he skips around a bit, but we settle into a long blissful canter, traversing the flank of the hill, gently descending, heading for the vale and home.

THE TEST ride had been a triumph up to that moment; I still then found it a great deal easier riding than walking. The sun had suddenly come out. During another lengthy canter I noticed that Dandy had a dark stalk that he had evidently snatched in a gateway dangling from his mouth, like half of Mr Foo Man Chu's moustache. He was trying to ravel it up with his lips, to eat it inch by inch and pace by pace.

It snapped off, trodden-on I think, and, as if to take it out on me, he broke into a gallop. But we came to terms by the time we got to the next gateway – he is headstrong, but not foolish – crossed the 'Top Road' again, by the old coaching inn at Lower Revels, long since a farm, and one of the handsomest farm-houses that I know.

Here we entered on a stretch of land that I cross by licence. The farmer, like many people hereabouts, was I believe bought into the world by my father, when midwifery formed a large part of a country doctor's work. For his, and no doubt for his own parents' sake, he lets me ride twice a week across two fields where I would otherwise have to travel half a mile of murderous road. The deal is that I don't have a dog with me - sadly no possibility of that now - that I take no more than one companion, and that we only walk or trot. For this inestimable privilege I pay him a small annual sum.

Soon we are on my immediate neighbour's land and within sight of home, but with, as it turned out, the most dodgy part of the ride still ahead. I had expected to be mobbed-up by his horses in Stonylongs, but was relieved to find the field newly full of ready-to-lamb ewes. But, half way along the field, Dandy suddenly dropped anchor, standing bolt upright at attention, staring ahead in the direction of the church.

It wasn't difficult to work out what the problem was. A white something-or-other was waving in the wind at us from the distant gate, some flipperty-flopperty thing that Dandy wanted to have nothing at all to do with. I pushed him forward, much against his better judgement, every bit on his toes. Luckily the wind eased briefly, long enough for me to open, manoeuvre him through, and fasten, the gate.

It was, as I had by then remembered, a notice about a footpath diversion that someone from County Hall had fixed to the post. Only a bureaucrat could affix such a hazard on a bridleway I unkindly thought, and he hadn't finished with us yet. As we turned onto my neighbour's driveway a sudden fresh gust set the wretched thing alive again, and Dandy bolted, his feet going in all directions on the slippery tarmac. As near as a touch he was down.

But we survived intact, turned into the home paddock, both of us blown-dry: his rug could go straight back on. Bella spotted us through her stable window and trumpeted her relief and joy – her world had not come to an end after all.

JASPER duly arrived with his mother and his latest thing, a pogo-stick, a couple of days later. Just as I take care to have plans for him, Jasper invariably has counter-plans for me. They usually involve amongst other things a run on any spare batteries I may happen to have in the house – it's a perpetual wonder to me how many mechanical toys children have now-a-days – but on this occasion I was down on his agenda to construct a car for him, just like the one in his current reading book, made out of an old orange crate on pram wheels.

I countered with my idea of clearing the rubbish in Kennels Lane. We soon struck a deal, and that evening sat down together and designed the 'Supercar'. "It looks a bit like a shoe" he said, but passed the drawing.

Next day, setting out in the Landrover we climbed to the ridgeway, and started to retrace my recent ride on Dandy in the reverse direction. The first object was to pick up a fence post with a lot of useful life left in it which I had noticed lying, discarded, a hazard, on Tess's track. If it should still be there, I had promised myself, we would purloin it. It was: we did.

Turning a blind eye to the rubbish on the main road – you have to draw a line somewhere or you would go mad – we dropped back into the vale parking at the end of the Kennels Lane furthest away from home. From then on, for two hours, covering in all less than a mile, we limped the vehicle from parking place to parking place, walking from it up one verge and then down the other, a hundred yards or so at a time, picking up as we went.

I used to do this job with Perdita, who could never quite enter into the spirit of it. But Jasper, who looks to inherit something of his father's build, was like a terrier, nipping into or under hedge or fence, whenever he couldn't reach or retrieve some offending object with my shepherd's crook.

"Must we stop?" he said, when I had had enough of it, and it seemed to me as if it were time for tea and home. We had collected eighteen pounds of rubbish I discovered when I weighed it on the stable scales, including thirty-two drink cans, and only half of the lane done: it doesn't bear thinking about... how the lane will look on one not too distant day. Does nobody care?

It was a very happy afternoon, and the best thing was we found an old abandoned number plate. If anyone reading this owns vehicle T582KAM, too bad: it's now the registration number of the Jasper Supercar!

WHEN Jasper and his mother stayed with us it turned out to be another of those weekends with a month's worth of events crammed into it. The Pope's funeral, the Prince of Wales's marriage, the Grand National and a Hunt Fun Ride all demanded and rewarded our attention.

Jasper helped me groom Dandy and then load him in the trailer for the Fun Ride on the Sunday morning. "What are those?" he asked, pointing to the chestnuts on his legs: you try explaining vestigial anatomy to a six-year-old. Later, during the last stretch of the ride, Jasper and his mother met me on the downland top, Church Hill, above Alton Pancras, with an irrepressible Lucas terrier Freddy in tow. Freddy used to belong to Jasper, but, a refugee from Hammersmith, he now lives in Dorset, the property of my companion on the ride.

This was a happy meeting for all concerned, except that Freddy, who gets about like quicksilver, suddenly, dashed to the full length of his extending lead under Dandy's belly, running out clear beyond.

It was a nasty moment, very typical of how, with horses, as with boats, things can so quickly go ludicrously and dangerously wrong. Fortunately the little dog elected to retrace his steps, returning by his outward route, rather than looping the lead round Dandy's legs, and perhaps bringing the four of us – dog, horse, man and boy – all down in a heap together.

Handing the dog over to his mother, Jasper accompanied me at a run for the last mile of the ride, fully earning the rosette which belonged to Dandy, but which I tied onto his arm.

Home again, I faced and lost a tussle with my conscience: it was the second Sunday of the month – evensong. The bells did it, there was no denying them, they got me to my pew. Jasper's hard-earned rosette was still in place when, to my surprise, he found his own way to church and joined me, shortly followed by his mama.

The first hymn was 604. Standing on the pew seat beside me, he soon got the hang of its catchy chorus, "One Church, one Faith, one Lord". But he fell asleep in his mother's arms during the less infectious later parts of the service. It had been a long day....

... and a long weekend. As we filed out of church the organist was playing "God bless the Prince of Wales".

DUFFY, our farrier, made a much better job of explaining 'chestnuts' on the morning Jasper left us, as I guessed he would. Until he arrived to shoe Dandy we spent time together in the carpentry shed; the Supercar seemed to have become rather my project, whilst he constructed a very realistic looking gun from bits and pieces in my oddments drawer.

"In the days of dinosaurs" Duffy said "horses were little things, with five toes on each foot. They walk on just the tip of one toe now, their hoof is a sort of fingernail. Those funny things we call chestnuts are just what is left of their big-toes and thumbs." "QED - well done Duffy!" I thought.

Last seen Jasper was halfway down the drive saying good-bye to the horses over the paddock railings, dressed as a crusader, armed, like the ghost in Hamlet, *cap-à-pé*. It's amazing, quite scary really, how unafraid of them he is, and how gentle they with him. They didn't seem to mind his visored helmet one little bit: neither party feels threatened I suppose. I went back to finish what I had been doing on his car.

IF MY two sons, Charles and Miles, don't feature frequently in these pages it is not because they neglect their father and their old home, but because they are family men, with busy lives to lead, one in the Midlands, the other in Japan. They visit us when they can, but seldom both together. At the end of January, a very sad exception had been the funeral of their mother.

Thanks entirely to her kindness and forbearance over more than a quarter of a century, we had kept on good terms: she had asked, when I last saw her, if she might be buried here. It cannot be often I suppose that one is involved in arranging the funeral and 'wake' for a former wife. It was daunting in prospect, from every angle, but not least because it would bring here so many who, understandably, might not be exactly glad to see me.

In the event the day went off better far than I could reasonably have hoped. The 'boys', will I ever stop thinking of them as such, of course did their parts from pulpit and lectern manfully, I felt extremely proud of them. And I, who had intended to occupy a back pew, found myself wanted forward. Nothing could have been kinder than my ex-in-laws, in the church and here at the reception afterwards.

It would be wrong to describe the occasion as being a reconciliation – we have never really fallen out – but for me it healed old wounds, self-inflicted, long ago: it left me feeling deeply grateful.

Before the party broke up we heard the happy news of another grand-child, my second, on the way.

NORMALLY one point-to-point a year is quite enough for me. I find them rather samey, and I prefer to meet my friends in ones and twos, rather than in droves. But this year I found myself attending four point-to-points.

We went as usual, out of loyalty and habit to our own meeting, it wasn't a good year to miss, with hunting on the rack. Work took me to two more – writing about the new thing, Children's Pony Racing, to which I am totally converted – then, the gang that we hang out with got up a party for another.

It was the old story, the serpent in this Garden of Eden, the same that got us to the Hunt Ball, beguiled my wife who is always game for a party, and before I knew anything of it another expensive car pass was pinned to the cork board in the kitchen, the date was in the diary, and extravagant picnic arrangements were in hand; it was a *fait accompli*, what could a mere man do?

It's not politic to admit it, else who knows what it might lead to, but I rather enjoyed the Cattistock point-to-point, in fact I enjoyed it immensely, and actually won some money on a horse.

Apart from the children's racing, what was new this year was that every now and then a total stranger would approach me smiling and nodding, possibly with hand extended. Was it the book I had recently published? Of course not; I kept forgetting the badge that I was wearing, which had a rather rude message on it for the Prime Minister: "Absolutely, quite agree" they would say, and "Where did you get that badge?". I've never felt so popular: oddly, no one has yet gone to punch me in the face.

Children's Pony Racing, in case you have missed it, is a facsimile of the real thing, without the jumps – a short dash over a few furlongs – the young jockeys otherwise going through the whole thrilling rigmarole of a race, including, especially, dressing up for it.

The idea, a brilliant one, is to engage and give a start to the young enthusiast in a profession dominated by the Irish. Who can doubt that it will be successful; I saw many promising would-be jockeys, mainly from racing backgrounds? But the joy of the thing for most of us I guess was to share the bubble and fun of the younger, sporting entries on their characterful ponies. Parents and grandparents were worth watching too.

Let's hope Children's Pony Racing doesn't get too serious.

"Whanne that Aprille with his shoures sote....
... Than longen folk to go on pilgrimages."

QUITE so, but I am not sure that I agree with Chaucer about April showers being 'sweet'. That may be a poet's view of them, as an outdoor man I find them a confounded nuisance. You have no idea how to dress when you leave the house, and the brilliant sun that takes you to the far end of the meadow, all optimistic in shirtsleeves to repair the fence, has given way to the wettest of wet downpours by the time you get there. 'Fox and goose weather' I have heard it called: there is no doubt as to which is the fox and who the goose.

But pilgrimages – yes? "Walk from 5 to 100 miles" the letter said, that came through our letter box in March, telling of us of a walk organized every year by friends of friends to raise money for cancer research. This year the walk was to start in Dorset, and reach Hampshire, in seven daily stages.

Still 'excused boots' as we used to say in the army of those lucky enough to be unfit for the parade ground, I could no more walk 5 miles than fly them, but the start-point was a place I particularly wanted to take a closer look at, and we had a friend staying who needed taking to the start. So the first Monday in April found us mid-morning at Nettlecombe

House, Cheselbourne – a house that hadn't been there the last time I was on horseback on that magic ground.

IF YOU lay a ruler on the map of Dorset, east-west, then north-south, you will find that the centre of the county is near enough Nettlecombe. It is just off a narrow road called Drake's Lane that runs like a strap over the empty downland and old sheep-walks between the shallow valleys that carry the River Piddle and the Cheselbourne on their way down to the Frome.

Riding home as a child, fagged out after hunting, I used to think it must be one of the longest and loneliest roads in the world, each crest never the last, and then at least 4 miles to go when and if you ever gained the Piddle valley road. As a man, owner of a horsebox, I have come to love it. It more-or-less follows the route that the monks of Milton Abbey must have regularly taken when they visited their brothers at Cerne, and vice versa.

Nettlecombe House, built in the Queen Anne style, over the past two years, by a scion of the family that named nearby Melcombe Bingham, stands the best part of a mile above Drake's Lane. You probably think that I am going to damn it as an intrusion, but I don't – I wish all modern houses fitted in to, complemented, their settings half as well. The 'meet' for the walk was well attended, walkers from all over, dogs galore, and off they all set.

My part was to meet them again at teatime at Child Okeford, and collect our houseguest. It was a brave sight, to see the small army trooping in off the ridgeway. I watched them, leaning on the top rail of a gate, feeling, and I dare say looking, a bit out of place, lost – I was off my own ground, amongst mostly strangers – when a young woman came and talked to me.

It emerged that she was the wife of an equine artist whose work I particularly admire, and with whom I once did a day's work, hunting. Her taking the trouble to discover my name, and then coming, introducing herself, and putting me at my ease struck me, and stays with me, as an example of something I really admire in those who have it… grace.

WHEN we eventually do get another dog it will have to be a lurcher, probably smooth-coated, certainly a bitch. It is a terrible thing to admit, but I am not a doggy person. Apart from a failed attempt by my parents to foster an unlovable black greyhound on me when I was still a schoolboy, Perdita was my first – Diana had had dogs before – and what particularly won my heart was Perdie's quiet grace, and, let me admit it, her cleanliness; I don't like hairs all over the house. That she worshiped me second only to her mistress, and regarded me as undisputed leader of the pack, clinched it.

Her arrival with us stirred my interest in lurchers generally, and I set about learning something of them. It's a controversial area, rife with real experts who have spent a lifetime devoted to perfecting lurcher strains, but I take for my mentor the late Frank Sheardown via his incomparable book*. I have become a bore about lurchers, I always fall back on them when at a loss for conversation at dinner parties, parading my new knowledge. But it does surprise me how little otherwise doggy people seem to know about them. So here goes...

The oh-so-fashionable lurcher, which we must be careful never to refer to as belonging to a 'breed', to be seen everywhere today in the smartest circles, is, like the cloth cap and denim overalls, a working-class thing taken up in these latter times by the leisured classes. What is now in many cases a cherished toy of the well-to-do has a near-criminal ancestry, being through centuries past the soul mate of gypsies, poachers and those hard men, long disappeared, cattle drovers.

The type is, in origin, extremely ancient, and essentially English. It goes back to feudal Britain and its fearsome forest laws, to the birth of our close countryside, our *bocage*, when the Saxon peasant, in order to fill his belly and thus needing to outwit his Norman master, invented a hybrid hunting tool that was speedy, tough and brainy, and did not break the ban on ownership of pure-bred gazehounds which was the exclusive right of lords and landowners.

The true lurcher, and here I am getting onto dangerous ground, but I hold fast onto Frank Sheardown's hand, is an intentional cross between a longdog and a herding, or working dog, or the offspring of parents so bred. A longdog may be a purebred greyhound, whippet, deerhound, borzoi, saluki, Afghan, pharaoh hound, Ibizan hound, sloughi, or a cross between two such.

Since the possible variety of working-dog out-crosses, stretching though every sort of terrier and shooting dog, is almost innumerable, it follows that the number of varieties of lurchers that can be bred, especially if one goes back to a longdog, as one should after the initial cross, is as good as infinite. It is great fun trying to guess the immediate ancestry of the lurchers you see at country gatherings, such as point-to-points, at least I find it to be so, and I have become quite brazen in asking total strangers about their dogs.

Only a few days before, at the Cattistock meeting at Little Windsor, there had been a nice-looking girl with long blond hair and three dogs on rope leads. She had a Jack Russell, a pretty brindled bitch of about Perdie's size, but skinnier, and a much bigger black-and-white dog that was evidently trying to be a lurcher but had not quite made it.

The bitch had the Doberman outcross and deerhound blood she told me (there must have been whippet in it also, somewhere, I was sure), and the monster was her puppy, by mistake, and by a neighbour's collie. She volunteered, what I had guessed, that a Labrador had something to do with it too. Such fun!

But that's quite enough for one lecture on lurchers: I shall remount my hobbyhorse later.

* 'The Lurcher – Training and Hunting' by Frank Sheardown – Swan Hill.

"TROUBLE?" I thought, at the sight of a neighbour from one the houses that back onto our meadow across the lane striding towards me as I was tending the bonfire one fine day last autumn. He had purpose in his look, was clearly not just out for the exercise, and, although we are the best of friends, not least when hounds are in the parish, wasn't likely to be merely wanting to pass the time of day.

Potential trouble it certainly turned out to be. If there is one thing that sets neighbour against neighbour round here in this wet vale, it is a problem with surface water, drainage or ditches – meddle with them at your peril, neglect them and you are damned. It's logical enough: it's about boundaries.

What this neighbour had on his mind was that the drain that should carry the wet from *my meadow*, under his ground and the lane to *my ditch*, was backing up, flooding his garden. There was I think also some ever so fleeting reference to his wife, who I suspect was watching our exchange from her kitchen window, which put an even more serious shade on things.

"Would I please do something about it?" he asked me, in the friendliest possible way – I promised to look into it directly.

There is nothing easier than falling out with neighbours. A suspected slight, an unguarded word, or a joke misunderstood, can lead to a lifetime of stand off and awkwardness; such fences, once damaged may not be easily mended. Country people are very proud, "As proud as Lucifer" my old mother used to say; it is a trait I both like and respect, even if I am wary of it. I will go to almost any lengths, turn any number of other cheeks, in order to keep on good terms with the people we live amongst. So I made a point of being seen inspecting the offending ditch before nightfall, and in a few days found time to start work there.

It was a short stretch of the paddock hedge, barely a rood, which, because of various obstacles, the mechanical hedge-trimmer couldn't get to. It had gone wild with bramble over the years, the ditch overwhelmed – I couldn't hope to see, let alone get to, the outflow of the offending drain, blind, some six feet down. There were two things to be done, clear out the bramble and other unwanted growth, and then lay what was left of the old hedge.

It took about three afternoons to clean out the hedge, chuck the rubbish over into the paddock, and make it up into a heap for burning. And if there is one thing that one needs to be even more careful about than drains it is bonfires, especially on Mondays: the wind would need to be strong and settled dead west before I could put a light to the heap.

When I eventually uncovered the drain I found that it was running sweetly. I am not sure that there weren't a few smiles at my expense up and down the lane at that, but, as Lizzie Bennet's incorrigible father asks in *Pride and Prejudice*, "For what do we live, but to make sport for our neighbours?".

I had certainly been doing my duty in the entertainment department. It had been amazing how busy people had been in the overlooking kitchen windows, quite unusual the number of walkers in the lane whilst I was at work. And very pleasant, it must be said, to break off for the occasional chat, and to accept the odd offer of help – "Here, let me get rid of that bit of bramble for you".

I AM not sure if I have mentioned that Dandy sat on me before Christmas? As March drew on, and the last chances to work on the hedge sped by, it was touch and go whether or not I could do it, but eventually I got out there: at least the heaviest part of the work, cleaning the hedge and dragging away all the dross, had been done. I just had a few pleachers to lay and peg down, and a bit of tidying up to do.

It is the simplest thing in the world laying a hedge, and lovely work: in fact there is nothing like it for engrossing the mind, making time fly, and creating something that will please every eye that lights on it. Who isn't delighted to see a hedge laid in the old style, rather than massacred by a flail?

All that you need is thick gauntlets, a sharp billhook, a bow saw, a pair of loppers (long-handled secateurs), and a supply of 'crooks'. Crooks, which you can cut out of the nearest hazel bush, are about the size of walking sticks, but with an acute accent instead of a curved handle.

You must decide first in which direction you are going to lay the hedge, this should be up-hill, if there is a slope, towards the sun if that is possible, or as seems most convenient if, as in this case, the hedge is level and runs due east-west. You select the first upright that you propose to lay, cut three-quarters through it a few inches from the ground, lay it, peg it down, trim off any twigs that do not please you, tidy up the wounded half stump where you made the cut, and move on.

There are two golden rules, one practical, the other one aesthetic. First there will probably be more uprights in the hedge than you need to lay, but never cut out any surplus living wood until you are quite sure that you do not need it: second, never use binder twine or wire instead of a crook.

ONE should not have favourites of course, but of our two horses, the chestnut mare Bella is my special pet and preferred ride. We 'bonded' very strongly several years ago when, on the day of the total eclipse, she fell in the road, damaged both her knees badly, and we nearly lost her.

Nursing her through that, with the endless injections and dressings, which she bore with such gentle, trusting patience, has made her very dear to me. Useless though she is as a hunter, or as a hack for Diana, I cannot think of parting with her – or indeed of ever parting her from her brother, they are so mutually devoted.

As an experiment we are working her barefoot, which is quite easy here, since we have ready access to bridleways, and several of our neighbours are so generous as to allow us the freedom of their land. I took her one early April morning to nearby Hay Wood to see how spring was advancing.

As always, she stepped away bright as anything from the mounting block. Although she howls like a banshee if I take Dandy away from her, under the saddle, faithless thing, she leaves him quite light-heartedly, apparently without a backward glance or second thought. There is a clue there somewhere to that fascinating but impenetrable riddle "How does horse regard man?"

A small rabbit sat crouching in our path in Stonylongs, barely bothering to move; and in the field across the road two roe deer watched us coolly for a bit, then ran off towards the wood, every now and then skipping high the way they will. I don't think I know anything more lightsome, beautiful than "the running of the deer".

In the wood it was too early really for the bluebells that would carpet the place, like the ground to a tapestry, by St George's Day – there were just the odd ones showing colour. The wood anemones were in their droopy cloche-hat mode, they would be dressed for Ascot later, once they have felt the full warmth of the midday sun. The wild garlic was no more than a smell, and the dog mercury, that ubiquitous undemonstrative little plant, also still all over green.

For the return trip, to make a circuit of it, we cut through the wood, ducking and weaving under and around the, overgrown, long un-coppiced hazel, where only the deer have easy passage. I used to bring the horses here a lot when they were youngsters, to make them more readily answerable to the rein, voice and leg.

Out in the open again, I give Bella a canter on the stubble. She floats over a small log that we reconnoitred on the way out. Unlike her brother, who is a bovver-boy and tearaway, she has a perfect mouth. I barely have to touch the rein, just saying firmly, in her ear, "Now Bella, that... will... do!" when I want her to ease up. Do you wonder that I love to ride her?

Back in Stonylongs again the baby rabbit still sits looking at us quizzically, not showing a jot of fear. Whilst a small vanilla heap by an exhausted ewe tells that lambing has just started, and heralds the most honeyed time of year: spring is truly here.

AS I was saying earlier... unlike purebred longdogs, which were ideal for coursing game in the open country, in saner times legally, under the eyes of the world, lurchers were originally bred for the hole-in-corner nefarious work of poachers and the like. Lurchers were, and in some quarters still are, demi-mondaines not to say criminals in the doggie world.

They were also bred, like foxhounds, specifically for particular country and particular work, and never for the showbench. There are as many possible types of lurcher as there are possible outcrosses among shepherds' dogs, terriers of all varieties, shooting dogs and even guard dogs.

Typically, a lurcher might be three parts longdog, to one part something else – ie the grandchild of the original nick. Some outcrosses one might describe as classic, such as that with the collie: some, especially the rough-coats, seem to be much more popular that others: some, like for instance the Labrador or Alsatian outcrosses, bred for killing foxes in Scotland as I discovered, come as quite a surprise.

Perdita, although I cannot know it for a fact since she strayed unannounced and uninvited into our lives, was, I have no doubt at all, one quarter Staff-ordshire bull-terrier, with half of the mixture whippet, and the remaining quarter greyhound. She had the front of a wrestler, the grace and body of a ballet-dancer, and no sign at all of that blunt, rather menacing, and, to me ugly, Staffordshire snout and heavy head.

Quite often you meet what I call 'would-be lurchers', dogs that are half way to the real thing, the result of the original outcross, probably expert breeders' discards, given away, their nephews and nieces no doubt poncing around somewhere as full-blown lurchers. I have a soft spot for these chi-chis, and am always glad to see that they have found a happy home, rather than being culled at birth – there is one I meet regularly on one of my daily rides.

But here I am banging on about lurchers, and I haven't told you the most important thing about them. Like much that is best in this country, they are of mixed ancestry, positively bursting with nous and hybrid vigour, and they have the sweetest nature you could ask for in a dog.

As my new lurcher guru, Jackie Drakeford, told me, "The only bad thing that lurchers do is get into our hearts and then leave us", and as she wrote in her gorgeous book*, "When the world is dark for you… your lurcher… will put her head on your lap and offer the most perfect, uncritical friendship and comfort".

* Jackie Drakeford – *The House Lurcher* – Swan Hill Press.

AMONG the less welcome harbingers of spring, along with tax returns, are reminders, sometimes from the pulpit, of looming Annual General Meetings and the arrival through the letter box of their agenda.

Just as there are otherwise sane and fastidious people who listen to 'The Archers', are amused by motorcars, have an interest in footballers and their antics, or enjoy water-skiing, so, I observe to my undying surprise, there are people who seem actually to enjoy committee meetings, almost to revel in them. How else can one explain why they endlessly prolong them?

Myself, I regard meetings of any sort with something of the same horror with which I anticipate speeches: you are a guiltless prisoner, to be released only at the speaker's pleasure, with no idea of when if ever your undeserved sentence may come to an end.

Who does not know the agonizing silence, always broken at the very latest possible moment, which follows the question "Is there Any Other Business?" Invariably, just when hope has so nearly triumphed over dread, a small voice, usually the same small voice, says "If I might just....?", and you know that, far from the meal being over, the main course is just about to be dished up.

The Village Tennis Club Committee meeting (I must tell you sometime about the Glanvilles Wootton Lawn Tennis Club, can you believe that such an important sounding entity exists in this tiny village?) is quite different from the others. It takes place in my neighbour's dining room, and there is usually a drink to be had.

There are less than half-a-dozen of us who manage the Club's business, usually dispatched in a matter of minutes, and who do the not inconsiderable work involved in keeping our court in good playing-order through the year.

This year we were joined by the cat of the house, a handsome Bengali with snow leopard markings called Mo Mo. He patrolled the table, stepping deliberately and in a stately fashion on everybody's notes, before hopping onto my lap and staring directly into my face with his fine, broad, blue eyes in the most flattering if rather disconcerting way. I seem to have become an object for cats: it's something new, I must try to get used to it.

The Church AGM, PCC and Village Meeting will certainly be dry, and catless, and I prefer not to think too much about them in advance. I shall no doubt fall back on the method I used as a schoolboy to while away lessons – wild, anarchic doodling in the margin of the agenda papers: I know that people see what I am up to, and that I am behaving badly, but cannot help myself.

During the long interregnum that followed the departure of my great friend, our old rector, and arrival of my good friend his successor – we have been unbelievably lucky in recent years in this group of parishes – it fell to me to chair the PCC.

It was my practice then, to make a parade of placing a small clock on the table in front of me before the meeting started. Since the agenda called for a prayer, I would ask the Good Lord to make the meeting, 'useful, harmonious and short', and then enquire what 'other business' members might want to raise at the end, making a careful note of the extra items on the agenda, so that we might all know in advance what extra delights we were in for before we might go home.

Both prayer and ploys were completely ineffective. What is more, it was made clear to me by some of those present, in the friendliest possible way – we have after all, most of us, known each other for the greater part of our lives – that I was being a spoilsport. Ah well! As they say in Yorkshire, "There's nought so queer as folk".

THE deep sigh that Dandy always gives when I appear in the stables with the saddle on my arm after breakfast is scarcely flattering, nor is the way he frowns at me. "Don't be cross" I say, or, to be entirely truthful, "Don't be cwoss", since, God help me, I tend to speak to him in baby language.

I give him a hug, all too reminiscent of the Judas kiss I gave his mother Daisy when I left her at the kennels all those years ago; for a moment I think of my own mother too, and taking her on her last journey to the Nursing Home. Why do things so often seem to end in betrayal – glum thoughts, must pull finger out, get busy tacking up and get on up the hill.

When I had collected the two of them from Chantry Mead first thing that morning, I had had a Wordsworth moment. Through the slightest possible veil of mist the skyline of the Heights looked breathtaking. Not "Ships, towers, domes, theatres and temples..." as the poet saw from Westminster Bridge, but Mount Sylva and High Stoy, with the dip at Dogbury in between.

To the left, in the foreground, Dungeon hill, and behind me the string of my neighbours' houses up the lane, leading to our place and the church and Church Farm beyond. All, however mundane in reality, was rendered beautiful by the low, early slanting sun and the diffused light. Bella banished Wordsworth with a push of her nose: "Get on with it" she as good as said, "We want our breakfast".

(Little does she know or care that I once got my prep-school Vth form early release from class by learning that sonnet by heart in a few minutes – how grateful one is for having been taught decent English decently.)

I don't have to look, but crossing the metalled lane Dandy's feet tell me that he still has a full set of shoes – Duffy is due again later in the morning – and barefoot Bella seems reassuringly confident on the hard surface. "No foot, no horse" they say; it's ever the first thought when I am bringing them in for work.

Bella had looked betrayed too, as she always does, when I pushed her face back to shut the loose box door on her; and the ginger cat – must find out its name – scuttled down the drive as Dandy and I turned into the paddock, heading for Dungeon.

LAST time out we had had an adventure. Returning from a recce of the Village Hall Outing, which I am to be responsible for leading this year, we had met a worried-looking group in the road – a motorbike, a prostrate figure projecting from underneath it, and a skinhead telephoning. Further on our milkman was busy scribbling notes in the cab of his van.

The skinhead assured me, very politely, with thanks for my enquiry, that he had things under control and didn't need help. But I made best pace home, urged Dandy, against his opinion of what was reasonable, through the wicket gate into the small, paved back courtyard and called for a thermos of hot, sweet tea. By the time I got back to the scene of the drama, the ambulance was there, shortly followed by the police. I drank the tea myself.

THIS time, I had two aims in mind, to find a spanner that I dropped up on the hill the previous summer, and to catch sight or sound of the ravens, which might or might not be nesting there.

I don't know which is stronger, the rage at losing things or the joy of finding them. I just dream of chancing on that spanner, although there has been hay taken from the field, cattle grazed on it through the winter, muck spread, and the hunt has charged up and down it half-a-dozen times, since I dropped it. It must be under the turf by now, but I can't help hoping, against reason, and praying fervently to St Anthony, that one day I will find it. Perhaps I shall see it sticking up out of the ground like a thighbone on an ancient battlefield; or maybe one of Dandy's shoes will tell me where it is.

The best part of a foot long, a shallow 'S', it must have been made by a blacksmith generations ago. I dare say some patient gave it to my father, as grateful patients would do when he noticed things. "Ye take it on home wi 'e Doctor, I've no use for 'n now" some old cottager, might have said, glad enough to make some return for his devoted care and tireless visiting. And now I've lost the precious thing: I can't forgive myself, nor yet forget it.

It was a gate at the top of the hill. Off at one hinge, a great nut needed easing in order to shift the eye back onto its hook. The job done, I had tied the spanner to a saddle 'D', but not carefully enough evidently. A couple of point-to-pointers appeared, doing fast work, and, wanting to get out of their way I dropped the hill quickly: it was gone when I got to the road. I don't know how many times I have been back to look for it.

No spanner, no ravens either on this occasion. I'd seen a pair of them being mobbed above a rookery in some Scots pines on the far side of the hill a few days before. Rooks are sitting now, hens tight on their nests, begging the cock birds for their breakfast, as thought they were fledglings, by shivering their wings. The rooks are in no mood to stand any nonsense, even from ravens.

And I had possibly heard a raven once, since, although one of my books tells me that a rook can make "a misleadingly raven-like croak". I know ravens visit Dungeon; I long to discover if they nest there.

I wasn't long empty-handed though. Up and back we had travelled Park Lane, as the narrow road that climbs the hill is rather grandly named. It has a steep bank on the old park side, no doubt it once carried palings; a sheltered sun-trap, it is like a nursery for bringing on every sort of hedgerow flower.

It's a simply lovely place, full of memories of hacking home from hunting in school holidays. But soon I was on my feet picking up hideous rubbish, beer cans and so on, and stuffing them down storm-drains, which is probably contrary to this and that regulation, but I couldn't either leave it, or carry it all home...

.... I promise to try not to mention litter in country lanes again!

Home once more, the horses turned away until Duffy should come, through the saddle-room window I saw Sooty sunning himself amongst the rows of house bulbs that I grow in the kitchen garden. I opened the door of Daisy's old loose-box, long since full of lumber. The old gladiator got up, stretched, and stalked in to see about the mice. More and more I get the impression that cats are in charge here now.

UNLIKE Mr Blair, I am not much enamoured of modernity. What can be more fatuous than always to be seeing a glimpse of eternal truth in the very latest thing; that is surely both the privilege and the folly of the young. We grown-ups ought to know better.

It is of course obviously true that each ticking second of our lives is entirely new; but it is also merely the growing point of an ancient plant that we need to study, respect and try to understand. *Semper aliquid novi...* said the Roman scholar and man of action Pliny, 'there is always something new....'. One can detect the two-thousand-year-old irony, imagine his raised eyebrow: he meant of course that there is nothing new under the sun.

These maundering thoughts were going through my head in early April as we waited in the chapel at the Royal College of Agriculture for the arrival of the bride, Clare, the daughter of my old and much valued friend our late Rector.

What could be more out-of-date, more primitive, than the old marriage service, when *at the day and time appointed... the persons to be married shall come into the body of the Church with their friends and neighbours: and there standing together, the Man on the right hand, and the Woman on the left, the Priest shall say...?* Yet what better way have we invented of marking, 'solemnizing', the most important turning point in life?

It gets worse... *Who giveth this Woman to be married to this Man?*... and David hands over his treasured daughter, whom I remember as a pretty child on her pony. I loath the way the media for ever go on about 'emotion', but truly it is quite difficult to play the man right through a wedding service, each word carries so much weight of meaning.

LIKE a school chapel, the one at Cirencester is laid out on the same lines as the House of Commons. So, instead of having to squint sideways at each other to get a view of 'the opposition', the bride's and bride-groom's people are face-to-face, and can inspect each other squarely across the nave. This is an excellent arrangement, cutting out the need for all sorts of stratagems, such as pretending to want to talk to an old aunt in the pew behind, or feigning loss of something or other. By the time battle is joined at the reception we have all sized each other up.

You would think that a seasoned journalist would never be without a pencil, and indeed I always have a supply of carefully sharpened stubs in the car, ready to slip into my pocket. But somehow, once again, I was without; as were my neighbours within whispering distance on either side. So my note on the service sheet is in smudged lipstick, I think it reads "1931-58 RJ Boutflower": the dates on the east window interested me, and the name appealed. What was the history of the college: I hadn't done my homework either?

I was to learn that this cradle of venery, whose beagle pack has launched so many on successful careers hunting hounds (I dare say Cirencester has done something for agriculture too) was founded in the mid-nineteenth century by enlightened locals, and consciously built in imitation of an Oxford college, with a quad and so on. The reception was on the college lawn, the wedding 'breakfast', in the upstairs refectory, my old friend's speech as good as any I have heard at a wedding.

Somehow I had got the timings of the day all muddled, I had thought that we were to be back in time to feed the horses, but it was past 10pm and inky dark when we eventually got home. Bella, so quick, unlike her phlegmatic brother, had heard the car on the drive and was at the gate to meet me bringing their belated 'tea'.

Dandy came at a gallop through the murk and joined us at the hayrack – it was rather scary, and his skid-stop, a flurry of metalled hooves in the mud, did no good at all to my wedding trousers. Serve me right for neglecting my poor horses, as I imagine you may be thinking.

The news on the car radio as we came into the village had been that the twenty-six-year pontificate of that great man Pope John Paul II had just ended. So Clare's wedding was an historic, as well as a very happy day.

THIS house is just made for giving weddings: even in winter there is no lovelier sight than the newly married couple coming down the orchard path together, under the over-leaning boughs of our picturesque, ancient, and quite useless, apple trees. The earliest wedding I can remember is my sister's, in November 1955 – I hope it wasn't on a hunting day.

We had a marquee on the lawn in front of the house, and the bride's health was proposed by an unforgettable character, the Commissioner of our Pony Club, General Sir Henry Jackson, with whom my sister was a great favourite, for her gutsy riding. The old warrior, typically, leapt onto a table, so as to be seen as well as heard by all: not a bad idea, I've not seen it done since. The marriage lasted until the last day of the year 2002, when my brother-in-law, a true friend, and one of the most admirable men I ever knew, suddenly died.

I had always supposed that when she married a boy from just a pony's ride away – it was a pony that first brought them together – that my sister and I would end our days living in adjacent parishes. But life is seldom so kind or tidy: she has returned to Australia, where they farmed for many years, and where their young family has taken root.

We are together at least in this book, for which she has kindly drawn most of the pictures.

AS I write this, it is St George's Day. Ten years ago yesterday I gave my younger stepdaughter away. The weather was just as it is now – a worry, wet and unseasonably chill; the daffodils have packed up early, the songbirds are sounding discouraged, tentative, and the paddock is more like a bog than a car park. But I think of it as one of the sunniest days of my life.

The great thing about being a stepfather is that you have many of the pleasures of true parenthood, but not all the responsibilities; at least, they don't seem to weigh so heavy as they might. It had been a wonderful thing, and great fun, suddenly to have two daughters, readymade, off-the-peg, in mid-life.

The only wobble from the bride, who is a cool customer under pressure, was over how her hothouse Italian in-laws-to-be would survive being frozen in the church. I said something, did something, I forget what, and the moment passed. Shall never forget though, waiting for her by the grandfather clock in the hall, just as my father must have waited for my sister, forty years before, and first seeing her on the bend in the stair, managing her veil and train.

There's nothing like an old-fashioned wedding.

NO WONDER it's called spring. Suddenly, in the dying days of April it went 'BOING!'. From a standing start, everything is in a flat-out gallop, especially the weeds and grass. From now on until 'the back end', as they say round here, the garden plays catch-me-if-you-can; it's half dream half nightmare, the grass being definitely in the later category.

To put a date on it, it was on the morning of 29 April, when, having saddled up the horses, I went to have a quick peep at the vegetable garden. The asparagus bed, which had been a pathetic sight just a couple of days before, was a forest of spears, you would think I had sewn dragon's teeth.

I am desperately behind with the garden. Some of my neighbours have potatoes showing above ground: mine aren't even in. I haven't bought a single seed. Must make a list; must get down to the garden centre; must get those spuds in, the compost spread, and the beanpoles up… today!

But I know I won't. There is a very military notice hanging on the drawing-room door-handle that reads 'War Room'; Jasper is down with his mama for his seventh birthday, there is a *playmobil* fire station to be built, and the Supercar to be completed.

One thing is done anyway, one seasonal milestone passed: Dandy had his rug off for the first time last night. And for the first time the horses' tails were on the go as fly swats, poor things, when I visited them this morning, as they will be on the go all summer: me too.

EASTER was unusually early this year, and we had spent it with the distaff side of the family in Italy, flying out on Good Friday, which was also Lady Day. This rare coincidence is said to bode catastrophe, and, indeed, disaster very nearly struck us.

It will perhaps come as a surprise to you to learn that I am rarely if ever late. Although I rather enjoy not wearing a watch any more, I cannot get out of the habit, either inborn or inculcated by an army life, of being punctual. Some people find this rather tiresome in me; others merely smile at it, as my nephews and nieces did when we rushed our breakfast, and departed my brother's Essex roof for Stanstead.

But even I had not allowed for airport shopping. "I must get something for Clare's wedding" Diana had said, dashing into a hat-shop, and reappearing with a small, fragile, hackle of purple feathers, which, as it turned out, it was to become my duty to cherish and keep out of harm's way through the next week of rough and tumble. Then, "I must get Louise a copy of *Tatler*", as she vanished for what seemed like an hour into WH Smith's.

If I tell you, without going into indelicate and unwelcome detail, that I discovered when we landed at Genoa that I had not yet refastened the belt buckle on my trousers, you will be able to work out exactly how I was placed when the Stanstead PA system called us forward by name, threatening to close our flight immediately.

As we struggled across the tarmac to the 'plane, juggling hand baggage, several Easter eggs for the grandchildren and Diana's most recent purchases, an important looking man in uniform – the pilot I supposed – was actually standing at the top of the ramp signalling violently and crossly that no-one else was to be allowed aboard. Fortunately he relented; but I shall never forget that panic at Stanstead airport, nor do I mean to allow anybody else to.

MY younger step-daughter and her husband live and work in Milan, but they rent part of a spacious and beautifully sited villa, two hours' drive away, just above the seaside town of Santa Margherita Ligure, on the matchless Bay of Tigullio (Italy, top left-hand side): we have become very attached to the place, and join them there at the least excuse.

So, just a few hours after the scurry at Stanstead, I was taking my ease in a favourite spot on their terrace, the same blackbird song that we had left behind in Glanvilles Wootton all around, the same camellias in bloom, though many more of them, a lemon bush in fruit behind me, and the familiar view out over the water to Rapallo twinkling away as the light failed. Bliss!

Italy I find to be the perfect foil for rural north Dorset. I am not so foolish as to pretend it has not got its darker side, its 'dark heart' as an ex-Sherborne Schoolboy recently described it in an excellent book*, but I don't have to endure its criminal and bureaucratic horrors, they are not thrust under my nose. I just enjoy the litter-free beauty of the place, the courtesy and charm of its people, their keenness to please, the kind weather, the dreamy food and drink, and the fact that *bella figura* rules in place of 'elf-n-safety, *aka* the Poison Dwarf.

* *The Dark Heart of Italy* by Tobias Jones: Faber & Faber.

ONE way or another round the year I get quite a lot of work done on that Tigullian terrace, but my favourite occupation is wandering down the hill to the town and its busy seafront. If I should have one or more of my step-grandchildren with me we will play football with the small inedible oranges that litter the steep spiral drive, kicking them down ahead of us as we descend.

Santa, as we all call it, is a place full of wonders and interest for all ages. I have always been a people-watcher, and have now become a dog-watcher too. I enjoy more than anything just strolling along, taking it all in, perhaps watching the catch being landed – Santa is still home to a small fishing fleet – or sitting at a pavement table, with an ice cream, a cup of coffee, or, if I am feeling expansive, a Bellini, that delicious champagne and fresh peach juice cocktail.

Whatever the season, I am always drawn to the churches, with their unbelievably ornate, and to my eyes, beautiful, awesome interiors. On Easter Saturday morning, in the church on the central piazza, they had not yet dismantled from the previous day a rough crucifix set up before a long white satin curtain in a side aisle to the south of the nave.

This I learned was for the ceremony of the 'Veneration of the Cross', proper to Good Friday. There were still worshipers coming in, kneeling in prayer before it, the women them moving forward to kiss the Christ's wounded feet, the men to touch them. I found it indescribably moving to witness, was glad I saw it, even though it always makes me feel a little jealous and guilty to see such unaffected piety, comparing it in my mind with what one sees elsewhere in our sadly godless world.

(How could I know that less than a fortnight later St Peter's Square in Rome would see the most remarkable mass demonstration of faith and reverence of my lifetime? We are still a powerful army, we who care about such things. And who would have supposed, even those of us who admire almost all things sunny, carefree and Italian, how faultlessly the funeral, and everything to do with it, would be arranged?)

I was only just in time. Soon, like the clownish figures in a Shakespeare play, gravediggers or whatever, whose role it is to bring the audience back to earth, two workmen appeared, and noisily dismantled the whole thing. Next day, when I was lucky enough to catch part of a service, the whole church was ablaze with arum lilies, and, I think, pink zinnias – I am no gardener, and am anyway largely colour-blind.

Outside, in the brilliant sunlight, a street market in full swing, it was like the opening of the second act of *La Bohême*: such liveliness, such life. There one had, just a few paces away from each other, the two sides of the bright heart of the Italy that I have learnt to love.

That afternoon I took myself off on my own to climb the hundred or so steps to the Church that stands above the town. It seemed completely to cure the lameness that I had been afflicted with since before Christmas. However tempting it might have been to think of this as a miracle, in fact I believe that I had merely stumbled on a form of DIY physiotherapy: I would certainly have not got past a vet on Easter morning.

OUR return flight from Christopher Columbus airport had this in common with the flight out, we were last to board – this time from choice – there had seemed to be no point in standing in a queue for a flight that was anyway an hour late, and for seats that were guaranteed. The effect however was that Diana and I were seated separately, I between a charming Italian student and a lady of quite different stamp.

It has been my custom through life, and as a countryman, to greet those I encounter; my attempt at this minimal pleasantry as I took my place next to her however met with cold disregard. Of about my own age, *soignée*, smartly dressed, she radiated *froidure*… and ill-breeding.

She was fast asleep when the stewardess came by collecting snack debris, later in the flight so, unasked, I disposed of hers. When she awoke, and I confessed the intrusion, she merely nodded her head, with barely a word of thanks. I last saw her, immaculate, pulling the smartest possible piece of wheeled hand-luggage, disappearing towards the passport check. I take my revenge on her by immortalizing her here as the 'Ice Matron'.

As we quit London's orbital motorway for the M3, well on our way back to Dorset, Diana said "It's funny, but I always think of Perdie at moments like this, when we are coming home".

SUMMER

MAY

"LOCKING up!... Locking up!..." I call into the empty church. It is the evening of May Day, and May is one of the two months in the year when I am responsible for unlocking and locking up the church. Six of us take turns to do what my old mother did day-in-day-out for all the years since the dawn of this repugnant necessity. What is a church for if you dare not leave it unlocked?

For the whole month's length it will be a daily problem not to forget the duty. Each night I will try to remember to place the massive key beside my spoon on the breakfast table, and each morning put it on one of the carved oak trays in the hall which, on another planet and in a different age, used to receive visiting cards, and where there is a good chance of its catching a passing, evening eye.

As well as being May Day it was, as you may remember, a Sunday – Rogation Sunday. The rest of the family had been on a Benefice walk, all seven of our parishes taking part, across the fields to the next village. But Dandy and I had played truant and gone on the 'Bluebell Ride'.

It had been slug weather that morning, heavy, close and warm. A night of thunder and illuminations had done nothing to clear the air, and the wettest April I can remember had done its final best to drown us. I don't know how many times through the month our ground had seemed to be at last drying out, and we thought "Brian will be round with the harrow any day now", and then another sousing put the notion back.

It was a strange, not very comfortable feeling, leading Dandy up the dank narrow path that winds under our garden wall, the 'way of the dead', to Church Farm, next door, to box-up for the journey. Almost to the day, playing hooky on another Sunday five months before, I had gone through the identical routine, on the way to a frightening accident and a spell in hospital.

Dandy, who had a 'Bollocks to Blair' badge fixed proudly at each side of his browband, seemed to know I was jittery – of course he knew, you don't have to 'tell' horses anything – and he was a bit boisterous and difficult to manage in the narrow space, especially while I was shutting two wicket gates behind us. An Arab running loose, flagging its tail and madly trumpeting in my neighbour's manège over the hedge didn't help: how much safer one is on a horse's back, rather than taking the chance of dodging his metalled, dancing feet! With Dandy boxed-up safe, it was relief at last to shut the tailgate on him.

The Bluebell Ride starts at Durweston, behind Bryanston School, just outside Blandford, and we through rode 15 miles of gorgeously varied Portman country, now in woodland full of bluebells, now on high open downland, now on the Ridgeway with colossal views. As we wound down off the hill through the edge of Blanford Forest for the last few miles, we passed three handsome groups of farm buildings, at Shepherd's Corner, Traveller's Rest and Websley, each rather sadly redolent of the wealth, strength and confidence of farming in another age. Then the impressive back-quarters and stables of Knighton House Preparatory School were around us; the ride as good as done.

The Bluebell Ride had not been an entirely profane alternative to the Rogation Sunday walk, a priest with guitar and small ring of choristers had been in attendance at the start. I felt quite cock-a-hoop as my kind neighbour drove us home – not least at having survived 15 miles on the back of a strong, opinionated horse.

As we turned into her yard, cascades of some familiar blue wildflower hanging down the wall caught the sun, and caught the eye, great beautiful long beards of the stuff. It's amazing, shaming really, how one can carry questions in the head for years without bothering to find the answers. I was determined, before the sun should set, to put a name to that old friend – it is called Ivy-leaf Toadflax, as I dare say every one of you already knew.

(For the record, and for the information of any reader unlucky enough to suffer a minor fracture of the pelvis, it seems that it takes exactly five months to make a full recovery from the injury, and that the best way to throw off the lingering after-effects is to go for a long ride.)

NEXT morning I rode Bella over Dungeon, my deceiving eye making a spanner out of every cowpat, and a raven out of every rook. As we came off the hill one large black bird was mobbing a middle-sized one, at a distance ahead of us in a gateway. I marked the flight of the larger bird to where it perched in the top of a still threadbare oak and rode up to it. What I had seen was no raven, but merely a carrion crow giving a hard time to a jackdaw – how difficult it is for the wishful eye to judge the size of single birds.

Crossing 'Park', as the field above the manor is called, you could see the Rogation Day walkers' tracks in the knee-high grass… well, knee-high to Jasper and his friend Jessica, who, along with the best part of fifty parishioners, had a wonderful time that morning, so he had told me.

Everything is suddenly 'up': I had seen the first Yellow Archangel in the roadside verge. It's like a nettle to look at but with flowers the colour of the worst sort of watery scrambled egg: my book describes it dismissively as 'creeping, hairy and strong smelling', but, as well as having a lovely name, it is quite one of my favourite springtime flowers.

Nearly home, I let Bella graze on the rampant cow parsley leaning over the drive – it needed trimming back. How horses love the taste of those succulent hollow stalks, it does one good to see and hear them enjoy scrunching them: and, as they chew, it smells wholesome, ferrous, and horsy-delicious. Bella arrived in the stable yard still chewing a long stork, like a slut with a dangling fag.

WHEN we had left home Diana had been busy on the telephone, "I'll just see if Julia can have kitchen supper with us, she's on her own this evening", Julia was my kind driver of the day before. She was still on the telephone when Bella and I got back. As it turned out we sat down seven to supper – eight, if you count Jasper, driven out of his bedroom by a bat – nine, if you count the irrepressible Lucas terrier Freddy, the same that had met us on Church Hill and all but turned a Fun Ride into a farce, running between Dandy's legs on his lead, a week or so before.

Freddy had been like a manic roller-skate before supper, charging everywhere, upstairs and down, barking a bit, overjoyed to be re-united with old friends again. It had quite taxed my sense of humour, when all one wanted was a quiet drink with old friends after a long day. But he's a dear little dog really.

Jasper and his mama departed next day, having stayed with us three days. But here's a funny thing you won't believe, never once did he ask me about the Supercar, which still sits half-made in the coach-house.

WHAT can be sadder than when an old friend becomes a bore, and having to tell it to "Shut up!"? You will have guessed that I am referring to the wireless, and what I still think of as the 'Home Service'. For over a month now it has had nothing to talk to me about except the beastly election. It was such a relief to arrive at polling day, and to be able to look forward at last to a reconciliation.

My mother, a woman of great character and strong views, always used to be the first to vote, arriving at the Village Hall spot-on 7am; woe betide the officials if they were not ready for her. I toyed with the idea of riding down to vote, but who would hold my horse? In fact I rode by, after voting, Dandy still displaying on each side of his bridle a rude message for the Prime Minister – I was tempted to take post outside the Polling Station like a household cavalry sentry, but funked it.

By lunchtime next day my valued friend was almost his old self again, and I didn't have to go forever twiddling for the Third Programme. The wireless has been an almost constant companion since boyhood, since I had my first study at school, and my mother said "You seem to like it so much, why don't you take it with you?".

I am not an uncritical friend. I deplore the general slant of the news programmes, which is urban, unpatriotic, and delights in nothing so much as the discomfort of the Royal Family. There are times when I just cannot endure bulletins, when they return again and again to scratch the same sore.

And who else but the BBC led the Gadarene swine over the cliff of political correctness, is still today the high priest of 'ism-ism', and continually forces medicinal doses of it down our gagging throats? But, time and again there are really good programmes, and one is gratefully reminded of how excellent, in my case, indispensable, the broadcast word can be.

Somewhere about the house I have a clipping quoting Arthur Ransom's dismay when the BBC started. He said, in effect, it would be the death of books, of imagination, of children making their own word pictures as they read. One can understand his fear, be grateful it has proved exaggerated, and just be a little cautious about making a similar generalisation, and the same mistake, over other modern wonders – like the computer I am using now.

I GO to church, much as I ride, out of habit – it is a part of my life that I value, part of my upbringing. Much as those of us who hunt do so for all sorts of different reasons, many having little or nothing to do with the serious business of venery, I wouldn't care to spell out exactly what going to church means to me. It's a bit of a muddle in my mind really, one can't expect to understand everything, can surely borrow faith from those who have it. Church feels right, that's enough for me.

For sure, one of the reasons for attending church is 'to support the parson', part of the glue of the village; another, dare I confess it perhaps my main inducement, is to hear and to repeat a form of the English language that is indescribably precious to me. When I read the lesson, it is quite a struggle sometimes to get through the familiar passages, particularly the New Testament, especially the parables, especially the Good Samaritan and the Prodigal Son. The words, the simple way that they are put together, the cadences, and the ideas they carry, mean so much, conjure up such clear pictures... of what one ought to have been, and ought to try to be.

Another thing is that one connects with history, local history, in church. A favourite prayer asks us to "Think of those who have gone before us in this place"; I do it the whole time when I am in my pew. One thinks of family of course, and past neighbours: Harvest Festival is particularly redolent of the still unbroken thread of farming in the village, and farming families that go back further 'in this place' than any of us.

But our most famous worshiper was a soldier, the First Duke of Marlborough. Brought to the parish as a baby, he spent his boyhood here. A recent biography would have it that his victory at Blenheim was what set Britain on her imperial path – it's a nice thought, our little village the cradle of empire. I tried to express this idea at the end of a dodgy historical jingle delivered at the Village Entertainment before Christmas: Blenheim, I declaimed ...

...was the tipping point in 'Our Island Story'.
Thus Empire, 'Land of Hope and Glory',

And 'Rule Britannia' all began
Thanks to one Glanvilles Wootton man.
So, when you hear it said
That once half the globe was coloured red;
That the sun never set on
Lands and peoples ruled by Britain;
Be sure to say out loud and clear
The British Empire started here!

Determined to wave a flag at the end, I had drawn the length of Cheap Street in Sherborne blank, including Woolworths, without finding a single Union Jack. Ending where I should have started, I asked my friend Ros Hole in the Joseph Weld Hospice charity shop if she had such a thing. She dived into the back room and produced six – given to the shop after the Queen's Golden Jubilee.

YOU will have gathered, or, to use a favourite Jane Austen phrase, you will have collected, that Bella, or Bluebell, to give her her full name, is nothing if not feisty. As I duck under the chain to get into her box to saddle her she often raises one knee sharply in a way that surely would earn her high marks in an unarmed combat class.

She will put all her full weight on each quarter in turn as I lift her feet to pick the hooves out, threatening to lie down if I take too much time about it, will gape like a shark at me when I secure her girth, and will wave her head around in a frantic gesture of non-cooperation when I go to put her bridle on. But she means no real harm. It's all play. In all her thirteen years she has never actually laid hoof or tooth on me – or if she has, I have forgotten it.

Once, and once only did she kick out, when I was clipping her and she was anaesthetised – it was an automatic reaction: the crack of her mailed foot against the stable wall was a frightening reminder of what harm a kick can do. I would never have a vicious horse in my stable – where's the fun?

But Bella is the horse that, however far away she is, however apparently happy grazing, will start to walk towards me as soon as she hears the field gate click, that never evades being caught, and that steps off so bonny from the mounting block.

IT WAS in part through Bella that I came to know and to admire the work of our local Horse Whisperer, Maya Horsey, a desciple of Monty Roberts, and trained by him in California. I had attempted to write an article about her mysterious art, optimistically entitled 'Seeing is Believing'. Had spent time watching her work, was well on the journey from my initial scepticism, when I decided that the acid test should be whether or not she could persuade Bella to load in the Rice trailer.

For several happy years we had used a horse-box, which Bella, since a foal, had, after a few dramatic and alarming interludes, been quite content to travel in. But when Diana gave up hunting the lorry became a luxury and had to go: nothing I could do would make Bella enter our new state-of-the-art, all singing all dancing two-horse trailer. Her brother Dandy made no difficulty at all about it, but, for Bella, its pokey confines just spelt out the one word "No!".

I am fairly experienced with this familiar form of 'nappiness' in horses, and reckon that I know how to deal with it. Most horses that are worth riding cannot be cowed or driven into obedience: kindness and endless patience is the only answer; but with Bella nothing answered. One afternoon I stood for hours trying to tempt and cajole her up the ramp – she might come halfway, but always ran back. The time came when I had to dress to go out for dinner, and I knew that the battle was lost... and lost for ever, you don't get a second chance.

When Maya came she first spent quarter of an hour moving Bella this way and that in our stable yard, every now and then stopping her sharply, backing her, rewarding her with a forehead rub ("Never pat, rub"). Bella answered by licking and chewing – the classical signs of submission – you would think she had read the Monty Roberts book.

"What are you doing?" I asked, as she and Bella then seemed to be 'setting' to each other as one does in an eightsome reel. "I want her to 'dance', read my movements and copy them: as soon as I walk away, I want her to follow me". This is what whisperers call 'joining up' I recollected.

Again, Bella seemed to be totally 'on message'. "See, there is no pressure on the line: she has chosen to be with me". Then into the trailer they went; no hoop-la, no fandango, straight in, walking, trotting, again and again. "I don't think there is a problem" Maya said with a laugh, handing the rope to me: suddenly there wasn't.

I didn't have occasion to put Bella in the trailer for a year or more after that, but when I did, she went in like a lamb. Does it surprise you that, as I wrote earlier, I look on our Horse Whisperer as something of a star?

AROUND the anniversary of VE Day the obituaries in the *Daily Telegraph* made particularly compelling reading. "What a man!" or "What a woman!", you would exclaim, reluctant to turn the page and read news of the dwarf doings of today.

On the Saturday of the sixtieth anniversary there were accounts of the lives of three recently dead ninety-plus-year-olds, a soldier, a sailor and an airman, the page dominated by a magnificent picture of a seated highlander, in bonnet, kilt and battledress. Lt Col Duncan Campbell had been commissioned into the Argyles in the year after I was born. He was serving with the Camel Corps of the Sudan Defence Force, when, heavily outnumbered, they bought precious time delaying the advance of the enemy on Khartoum, in June 1940.

He "was ordered to guide two companies of infantry onto a strong Italian outpost position. Walking ahead of the infantry, Campbell (who was well over six foot tall) ensured that his CO did not lose sight of him in the rough terrain by singing… at the top of his voice amid the crack of rifle bullets and the noise of shell explosions."

Afterwards when "asked whether he wished his name to go forward for a VC. He replied that he had done nothing to deserve it". Later in the campaign "when told that he had won a Bar to his MC, he called his men together and placed the award around the neck of each of his soldiers in turn".

It was something of a shock to learn that Duncan Campbell had settled in Dorset when he retired from the army in 1949. "Where?" I wondered, how had one never before heard of this heroic giant of a man? The telephone directories were no help. Invited out to supper and lunch – Diana was away being a grand-mama in London, and kind neighbours know how insatiably sociable I am – I asked everyone I met: blank everywhere, at church on Sunday evening too. No one could tell me of Duncan Campbell. It's an old story, these World War II heroes just live out their lives modestly amongst us: we only learn about them when they die.

AS I had left the church after locking up on that same Saturday evening a new notice in the porch caught my eye. It read "The Parochial Church Council found several tomb stones to be in a dangerous condition at the annual gravestone inspection; and so they have been laid flat for safety. The known relatives have been notified etc etc". This is of course the Poison Dwarf at his nasty nosiest and silliest in operation; he would have us all in thrall, and the poor old PCC, and busy unpaid Church Wardens, have to jump when featherbedded officialdom says "Jump!".

Who knows what ramshackle and expensive Heath Robinson system of bureaucratic wheels, cogs, belts and pulleys, connects some airless London office with our little churchyard, so that it can lay its inky finger on our PCC? Perhaps that is what is meant by 'outreach', a word so beloved of the meddlers whose salaries we all pay so that they can make a nuisance of themselves. Why can't they just leave us alone to run our own parish affairs, as we have since time long forgotten?

And what a weird paradox it is, a government that sends bombers across the globe, indiscriminately to blow Serb and Iraqi women and children to bits, interests itself in the billion-to-one-chance of a tombstone suddenly falling on a passing tot in North Dorset. Stranger almost, it can send our troops here there and everywhere, but it cannot for instance even deploy one policeman in the churchyard of St James's, Rochdale, where one read that week-end "the teenagers have taken to loafing around... smoking dope and swigging alcopops", and where "sometimes they throw stones and eggs at the windows, and thunder up and down one wing of the church".

What have we done, where have we gone so wrong, that this once warrior nation has allowed itself to be enslaved by petty dogma, by a detestable top-hamper of bureaucrats and political Nosey Parkers that would put us all in bibs and pinnies, make infants of us, crib and cramp us, take away every precious freedom, licence our every word and breath? I sometimes think that we are like Gulliver, pinned to the ground by midgets in our sleep: I long for the day, as surely must come, when we will eventually rouse and shake ourselves free.

I ALWAYS get into scrapes when Diana is away; I'm not fit to be left alone really, I wish that she would understand that. That same week-end, I had asked my old friend the organist to come and have supper after evensong, so that she could talk to me about walking puppies – a saintly duty that some people do for the hunt (once, long ago, was quite enough for me). I had to write about Puppy Walking for *Horse & Hound*, had as usual left it too late doing what kind people call my 'research', and was in the usual blind panic to meet a deadline.

Evensong is quite my favourite service, although I curse a bit sometimes when the bells start, I've forgotten it's the second Sunday of the month, and I'm still in my Sunday-worst. On this occasion however, only just back from a lunch party, I was already suitably dressed.

It was a gorgeous evening, a blackbird adding its song to the quieter parts of the service, but my peace of mind was destroyed during the General Confession when I was reminded that I had left undone something that I ought to have done – I had failed to put the potatoes to bake in the oven for supper.

So, Margaret the organist had bread and butter with her cold meat and asparagus, but she deserved no better. She, the widow of a Master of Hounds, had nothing of any use whatever to tell me, except that a beagle puppy had once eaten her favourite fountain pen. She did however say "Try *Who's Who*", when I asked her about Duncan Campbell; but I drew all five pages of Campbells in that invaluable volume blank – there was no mention of that modest man.

NEIL, the young farmer who makes hay on half our pasture every year in return for grazing the two orchards, has just delivered his rams for their summer holiday. I name them, Rambo, Rameses, Ramillies – in honour of Glanvilles Wootton's greatest son – and Blunkett. The last-named does not see too well, but is clearly still fit for work.

The rams for some reason never seem to welcome holiday time as you or I might, and break out of the lush orchard given half a chance. Diana and I were having supper on the Monday evening, I having just collected her from the station. We were discussing the ways and means of her returning to London the next day to change a jacket she had bought that was the wrong size, when Toffee's owner, the gamekeeper, came to the door. "Your three boys have just walked down the lane, I've shut them in the small paddock" he said – what a kind neighbour, actually to run to the rescue and do something about the problem, rather than just pick up the telephone!

"Couldn't be ours, we've got four rams" was the first complacent thought, but a trip to the orchard told a different tale. Poor Blunkett couldn't find his way to the gap the others had forced through the hurdles, and wouldn't be driven to it. There was nothing for it but to leave him there, take a bucket of water to the three escapees, and ring their owner. I make it a rule not to meddle with the rams, unless I know them really well.

I haven't told you about Toffee have I? He's the ginger cat that is always running away from me when our paths cross in the garden, and I sometimes almost mistake for a fox. Discovering his name was one of the useful things to come out of last week's Village Meeting; that and the fact that he often brings a baby rabbit home. Although he still won't talk to me as Sooty does, he's a welcome trespasser.

IT WAS in the middle of Hay Wood next morning that I thought of the Westminster Retable, that miraculously surviving altarpiece, then on display, or so I believed, in the National Gallery. Why should I not take Diana's jacket back to Knightsbridge, and then go and see this medieval wonder; I could scribble about hound puppies in the train, where better?

We were on an egg-run, Dandy and I. In the previous few days the ground had changed from bog to bone, suddenly, the way it will; tractors were out, feverishly ploughing, and the air was full of scent of drying earth. We'd lost the stubble canter, but the wood was at its loveliest blue-bell best.

Metaphorically putting spurs to Dandy, I zoomed home via the chicken farm, flung on London gear, scooped up the precious Zara bag, writing stuff and a map of London, and roared round in the car to Church Farm, where Diana was at her weekly Italian lesson.

"Scusi, scusi, momento, padonnèz moi... etc" I said, bursting into my neighbour's dining room, and showing off my fluency to my old Italian teacher. I explained my plan, in English, got it reluctantly approved, and just made Sherborne in time for the next up-train. The station had been at the mercy of voluble and mildly alarming young drunkard or drug addict on the previous evening, and the down-train late, when I had gone to meet Diana, but now it was at its spick-and-span, obliging best. I don't believe there can be a better-run railway station in the land.

I love travelling in trains – if only they could just go in circles instead of taking one away from home – I don't know a more congenial place to work. Scribble, scribble I went, with "Yes please!" at every chance to the man with the mobile buffet, and "So sorry!" to the lady opposite, as, for the umpteenth time I kicked her foot in my distraction. Salisbury, Andover, Basingstoke, Woking... in no time we were at Waterloo, with the only really tricky bit of the journey yet ahead, the underground.

I must have walked several miles under the capital that morning, certainly my longest walk since Dandy sat on me – ever tried getting to the Jubilee line from Waterloo, and then to the Piccadilly line at Green Park? – I had clearly gone the wrong way about getting myself to Knightsbridge. It would have been a comfort but a delusion to suppose that I would know better next time – I am always lost in London, always forget how it was I went adrift last time.

"Zara is just opposite Harrods" Diana had said, which meant to me on the far side of the Brompton Road. I crossed over and headed west, not a sign of Zara. "Lancelot Place – nice name, wonder how it got it?" I mused, Montpelier Street, still no sign. A nice New Zealand girl sitting at a pavement table gave me the about-face, "I'm sure it's that way", she said, indicating the direction I had come.

No point in asking a man the way to Zara: a well-dressed lady in the American Express office, looking puzzled, pointed across the Brompton Road to where the place announced itself for all to see in four-foot high black block capitals. It was immediately beside the entrance to the underground, where I had emerged, a blinking mole, a quarter of an hour before. "Opposite Harrods" evidently meant across Hans Crescent – silly me.

The business with the jacket done, I looked for a five-pound lunch, and settled for a ten-pound sandwich in the Knightsbridge Café, in William Street. Nice place, full of shoppers, plotters and lovers – how I enjoy eavesdropping, building pictures out of stolen fragments. I was looked after by a smiling Nepalese waiter who brought me white wine when I had ordered red – I drank it.

Finding the entrance to the National Gallery posed an Intelligence Test, which I failed. The familiar portico was boarded-up. Working round a flank I found what looked like the tradesman's entrance where another nice lady – it was a day of nice ladies – admitted me.

She told me that the Retable exhibition was not due to open for a fortnight, and that the earliest time I could get to see the Caravaggios was teatime. Frustrated, and furious with myself, I dived into the interior thinking at least to take a peep at the Reynolds portrait of my mother's illustrious ancestor holding the keys of Gibraltar, got lost and fled.

So much for my unplanned, ill-considered, snakes-and-ladders day in London: perhaps you will have sensed that I don't feel entirely at home there? I know that as an Englishman I ought to like and be proud of the place. On a fine day, as that was, and when everybody is smiling and helpful, as they were, I almost do like it; but I am for ever scheming on the quiet to catch the next train home.

Throughout the day I had carried a nightmare in my head. It's an acknowledged fact that I am absent minded; much more so now Diana tells me since I have been taken up with writing. Going up to London, and coming down, I had been haunted by the thought that I was fated to leave the Zara bag somewhere, on the luggage rack in the train perhaps; or that by negligence I might allow it to be stolen.

That evening I was more than usually happy to get myself, and the precious package with its much value-added contents, safely home.

THEY laughed in my face when I asked for seed potatoes at the Garden Centre, but some kind soul located half a sack of them unsold. They weren't the sort I wanted, but I took them gratefully home and hastily buried them.

One of the disadvantages of looking over people's hedges as you ride, is seeing how virtuous and betimes your neighbours are in their gardens, and being reminded how behind the game you yourself are. Oh well – at least my potatoes will not be troubled by the late frosts we have been having. The beans are in now too, and most of the seeds that ought to be: it's amazing what you can get done in one dry afternoon.

All the time I was working in the kitchen garden I was aware of poor Blunkett, still in solitary, just over the fence in the small orchard: it doesn't seem right to leave a sheep on its own. I gave him the old broccoli stalks to strip, which he seemed to relish. We have become quite friends; he asks to have his face scratched when I check his water each morning on the way to unlocking the church. I hope that Neil comes to reunite our little flock soon.

AS sometimes happens, on the next free afternoon I was kidnapped, and carried off in captivity for some slave labour in the flower garden. I enjoy growing vegetables but have no patience with flowers, they are so precious, untidy, un-soldierly you might say, and so often disguise themselves as weeds. You know where you are with vegetables.

And the weeds in the kitchen gardens I almost regard as friends; at least I know them when I see them. I'd be quite sorry if they were suddenly abolished – under some miraculous New Labour target perhaps, like death or poverty, reduced by 90% in the next x years or whatever.

I suppose they all have names, but I know most of them just by their natures. There are those rather pathetic, quite pretty, frilly ones which have no roots at all, and which you can gather in handfuls, and at the other end of the weed spectrum there is the one that I call 'the tick'; a squat thing with grasping claw-like roots that you have to take really seriously, treat individually, put a fork under if you want to shift.

King of them all is of course bindweed, first met as convolvulus in the nursery in some fairy story. How satisfying it is to draw out one of those long white naughty burrowing roots. I should be really sorry to exterminate the bindweed, I regard it as a worthy adversary.

Until recently I used to put all the weeds, except for bindweed, on the compost heap, but have been reluctantly persuaded by various experts that this is not a sensible thing to do. Instead I take the greatest care to ensure that not a scrap of vegetable waste from the kitchen fails to end up there – especially pineapple tops, avocado skins and so on. Mine is truly a multicultural compost heap, one that must surely bring a blush of pleasure to the wan cheek of even the most serious *Guardian* reader, and curl his sandaled toe.

My exile to the flowerbeds is not always without reward. As usual, on this occasion, it consisted mostly of moving clumps of this, that or the other from here to there, and, as often as not it seems, back from there to here again – very confusing for the poor things it must be. The latest news is that I am to move the fig tree; that will have to wait now until 'the back end'.

And again, as usual I was required to sacrifice some of my precious compost, and do a bit of serious digging. Once, a year or so ago, I turned up a small napped flint tool in one of our flowerbeds: to this day I keep it by me as a talisman. On this occasion I found a small grubby, wooly 'thumb', a lamb's tail, no doubt brought in from Stonylongs, intended for a bird's nest but discarded.

WE MEANT to ride this morning, but it dawned chill and wet. With Miles, my younger son, due for a visit from Japan, it seemed sensible to let the horses rest idle for the day, not even bring them over to the home paddock.

But they had a different notion – what contrary creatures horses can be. When I went just to check on them, to say "Good morning", and give them each that little something that I always carry in my pocket… and which they know I carry in my pocket, instead of being at the very far end of the field, as they surely would have been if I had wanted to bring them in, they were standing at the gate, saying, as clearly as if they could actually talk, "We want to come over please. If you don't mind and it's not too much trouble; we would like to stick to our usual routine".

So there was nothing for it but to go back to the stable, fetch the head-collars, and bring them across the lane. They made straight for the chest-nut trees, now in full generous bloom, to pretend they were giraffes and graze on the lower branches. Again, they were as good as saying "Thank you. This is precisely what we had in mind".

MILES'S visit was a great joy. He heads up Associated Press's Television News bureau in Tokyo, a job that takes him with a camera crew, at no notice, to wherever the breaking news is in that far quarter of the globe. Without knowing it, you will have seen many of his pictures. When the tsunami struck he had, straight away, to find and hire a 'plane, and get himself and his team down there. It's an adventurous life.

He came to us fresh from achieving a world scoop, by getting to hold a conversation – it lasted some eight hours – with the notoriously reclusive chess player Bobby Fischer. Talking himself onto the 'plane that took Fischer on his escape-flight from Japan to Reykjavik to evade extradition to a vengeful USA, Miles secured the multi-phobic oddball genius's confidence, and got the precious interview.

Miles, who is no paparazzo, had from the start decided that it was to be done honestly or not at all, and there was a big gamble involved – his flight would cost AP many thousands of dollars. The trickiest moment came when Fischer learned our name, so often thought to be Jewish – it is in fact Scandinavian as a helpful Swedish airhostess was able to assure him – and the breakthrough came when Miles was able to give Fischer his own share of Baileys liqueur, strictly-rationed evidently, even to First Class passengers. When we asked what his new friend looked like, Miles replied "a cross between Father Christmas, a homeless man and God".

WITH Miles's help, the three of us managed to shepherd the three R's back to the orchard to rejoin Bunkett. But there was apparently no pleasing them; whilst I was pottering around by the orchard that evening, after Miles had left, a loud 'twang' announced that Ramilles had hurdled the sheep wire. He stood looking at me quizzically before starting to make off, intent apparently on sampling the sweets of the kitchen garden.

It's amazing what you can do when your dander is up – I was really cross. I wouldn't normally dream of handling a strange ram, but I bundled him back through the wicket gate by main force, gripping his wool and pushing him in front of me: luckily his after-end, his daggings, were not too disgustingly disreputable.

I think that I had taken both of us by surprise, and it seemed to have taught Ramilles a lesson. There has been no similar trouble since, but I have come to understand that the rams are best left alone, that it is wisest not to engage their attention, not to meet their eye, at least until they are more settled. I squint at them once or twice a day from a distance, probably from a window of the house, when they look a bit like disgruntled rhinos in an enclosure at Whipsnade. They seem to want to join me if I hang around the orchard, they challenge the fence, test its strength with their considerable weight.

They will be altogether quieter, less itchy-fidgety and nicer to know, once they are shorn.

TOWARDS the end of May my summer job, writing about the game of polo, comes round once more: for some time now I have reported the main high-goal matches of the English season for *Country Life*. Unlike my winter job, writing about hunting, which I do from the saddle, and when there is usually plenty of action to describe, polo-writing is something of a challenge – one match is much like another. Polo is really a game to play not one to watch, let alone read about.

However, the work is fun, well paid, and I have been grateful for it: also some *Hello* style hospitality is occasionally thrown in, which, once in a while, we both enjoy. But each year recently, as I have driven back to Dorset yet again from some distant polo ground on a Sunday evening, with a deadline to meet first thing on Monday morning, I decide I've had enough of it.

I've 'retired' twice to date, but it doesn't seem to stick: any day now comes the Prince of Wales Trophy, at the Berkshire club, the first major final of the year. It seems to be a case of 'here we go again'

I FIRST learnt to play polo with my regiment, in Malaya. It's highly addictive. Once you have struck that ball, seen it soar away, galloped after it and by some lucky chance struck it again you are hooked beyond hope of recovery. For some twenty years, in season, I thought of almost nothing in my leisure time but playing polo... the next game, the next match.

We were not a moneyed regiment, but in those days it was permitted to employ soldiers in the stables, and we had our own army farrier, so there was just the fodder to pay for. Keeping a brace of ponies was well within the reach of even the most impecunious subaltern, especially if he didn't run a car. And again, in those days, playable ponies could be bought second, third or fourth hand, poor things, for hundreds rather than thousands of pounds.

When I finished with regimental soldiering on giving up command, I gave up polo too, and presented all my kit for distribution amongst 'the poor': this proved to have been premature. Languishing somewhere on the staff a couple of summers later I received a message "Will you please present yourself at Tidworth to play for 'the Old and Bold' against the Regimental Team?".

Picture the scene when we parked on the edge of the beloved and storied Fisher ground at Tidworth. Two ponies, in the care of a groom whose face and name I knew, appeared from somewhere, as if by magic. And then the real miracle; from various directions, un-summoned, came sundry presumably penniless subalterns, one bearing my hat, one a bundle of sticks, one my old boots, one my kneepads. "There's manners for you" I thought, who had cared probably more than I ought about my regiment's reputation for friendliness and good manners.

For some reason, although a complete rabbit at games, I have found that, just for a few honeyed moments, when I come back to a sport after an absence, and before I start to think about how I have been taught to strike the ball, I have a brief moment of carefree brilliance. It used to be the same when I played tennis.

So it was, that in the opening moments of the first chukka – they had kindly allowed me to play in my favourite place, at back – the ball lay almost on the centre spot. Cantering through the ruck I struck it, it soared, exactly bisecting the two distant posts. It was the fluke of a lifetime, and we won that close-fought needle match by just the margin of a single goal – my last.

High, but trying not to speed through Shipton Bellinger on our way home, I heard Diana say "Darling, wasn't it just **sweet** of your old regiment to let you score that goal?".

MY professional dealing with polo clubs would generally be through a Public Relations Officer, almost invariably a blond girl called Samantha – although I have come across rare exceptions to this rule. So when I was negotiating details of a working trip to Florida I assumed the voice on the end of the transatlantic line belonged to someone out of roughly that same stable; although something in the timbre of the voice did counsel doubt.

I had played hard to get, only agreeing to go to Florida on the condition that Diana came with me – money was no object, and we were royally, and very kindly, looked after. But the great surprise came when we were collected from the airport at Miami for the journey of well over 100 miles by road up the coast to Windsor, in Indian River County. The driver asked did we know Mrs Lambert (the PRO), were we aware who she was, and that she was 92 years old?

Eleanor Lambert was to prove one of the most remarkable, and engaging women I have ever met. She died, a centenarian, two years ago; I am looking at her *Daily Telegraph* obituary as I write. A daughter of the sawdust ring – her father was 'advance man' for Ringling Brothers' Circus – she was to be intimate with every President's wife from Eleanor Roosevelt on, to invent the International Best-Dressed List, and to rule the American fashion scene for more than half a century.

Our last communication from her, a fax from her New York apartment on East Fifty-eight Street, reads "Your letter.... Made me feel nostalgia for the peace, quiet and birds of Windsor... Affectionately, Eleanor." Peace, quiet and birds indeed; Windsor, established in the 1980s by Galen Weston in old citrus groves blighted by a freak frost (it shares a latitude with the Sahara) gave us a heavenly week.

It had been an enormous thrill to leave Heathrow on a dreary winter's day, and to chase the sun west – business class! To arrive in darkness and – no one had told me about the birds – to see a great blue heron, an enormous creature, flap idly across my field of vision as the sun rose next morning. Then, wonder of wonders, an osprey patrolling a stretch of water, ibis, with their improbably beautiful plumage flocking on the polo grounds, along with killdeer and other waders that I could not name, all unbelievably tame, unafraid, apparently unperturbed by man.

It was a short walk to a beach, public property but of an emptiness, extent and beauty that took the breath away. Here there were pelicans, and sanderling scuttled round one's feet, alternately chasing and being chased by the waves' outrun. If the wind was up, small black palmetto seeds would scurry along the white sand with blithe brainlessness, seeming to be rushing to something or other, like Lewis Carroll's oysters; if the tide laid them low they would wait until the sun had dried them, then jump up again and off.

The highlight for me were the exotic birds; for Diana a tennis coaching session with Ivan Lendl. I had never supposed when I picked up the telephone a dozen years ago and said "Yes, I had played polo... yes, I suppose I could have a go at writing-up a match", that it would in due course take me for the first time in my life across the Atlantic to see my first osprey, and to make a friend of the doyenne of American *bon ton*. Polo-writing has not all been fizz and flannel.

"I'VE 'EARD different" a much-loved ranker Field Marshall, Sir William Robertson, who died in the year I was born, is said to have growled when he didn't believe what he was being told by a smart young guards officer on his staff. Our gnarled old ash tree seems to be saying something similar to me – it stands completely naked still, at the end of May, when every other tree in sight is fully clothed for summer. If the old country saying is true, that wise old ash may also be shouting "Drought!": we shall see.

I have been writing about May as if it were a part of summer, but truly, this year, it seems to have been the rearguard of winter. Apart from a few warm days at the beginning, when I dispensed with poor Dandy's rug, it has either been dry and cold, with the wind set in the northern quarter, or, as it is this morning, blowing a wet gale from the south... and cold with it. Luckily Dandy seems to have acclimatised, and I don't feel too bad about the rug. He seemed happy enough when I visited him this morning.

It was on a day like this that my mother once found a buzzard sheltering in the church porch when she went to lock up one evening. I have had no such excitement. Swallows have built in there, as they usually do, to the Wardens' great annoyance, but I am not sure that they are really serious about it. Quite often, as I walk into the porch, one of them flies out, nearly brushing my cheek as we both pass under the apex of the low arch. But I haven't seen either of them actually sitting.

One Monday morning there was a bat lying spread-out and looking a bit sorry for itself on the stone seat that runs round inside the porch. I gave it an illegal poke with the church key. Bats, like badgers, have friends in high places and, unlike a mere taxpayer or property-owner, have a direct line to the law, you can be prosecuted for inconveniencing them. They are a great nuisance in the house: Diana won't rest when one them is loose in the bedroom, causing me to rush around with a tennis racquet and gardening gloves when I had much rather ignore it and go to sleep – I don't much like bats.

When I gave it a prod it moved, my guess was that, like us, it had come out of hibernation too early, was regretting it, and had gone back to sleep. My *Fauna Britannica* says that "bat identification is never simple... and ... tends to rely on... such elusive characteristics as ear length, pattern of teeth and length of penis". Ear length was enough for me: I reckoned this was a Common Pipistrelle. (Why is it that our so exciting wildlife and wild-flower discoveries are always dismissed by the experts as 'common'?)

THROUGH much of the month I came to think more and more about that bat, began rather to like it. Usually it was hanging, looking like a smashed umbrella, clinging by its elbow-claws to the napped flint wall of the porch.

One day when it seemed to have disappeared I found it hidden behind some paper pinned by its corner to the frame of the porch notice board. It was a copy of that same notice that some dafty from County Hall had pinned to the gate into Stonylongs, and which had given Dandy such a fright a month before. "Is my bat a bureaucrat, sheltering like that behind a piece of paper" I wondered, "it certainly knows who its friends are?".

Then one Sunday, after morning service, it had shifted back to the stone seat where I had first found it. The Rector looked grave and shook his head, and, sure enough, that evening, when Diana and I got back from a happy day at the Quantock Staghounds' annual lunch at Pontispool, which is not as you might suppose in Wales but just the other side of Taunton, it was lying like a murder victim spread-eagled on the porch doormat.

I went out early next morning – I would like to say after a sleepless night, but the bat had not got to me quite that seriously. Some questing nose had turned it over during the hours of darkness; 'batty-bat', as I had come to think of it (remember that silly song?), was on its back undeniably dead.

Picking it up by one of its single wing-claws I carried it to the carpentry bench, got a magnifying glass, and had a good look at it. Its fur, not unlike a mole's, is quite attractive, tan on its back, light brown and woolly underneath. The unexpanded membrane of the wings looked a bit like Persian lamb, inky black and crinkly, and it had five identical, rather menacing claws on each hind foot. But its face, in repose, eyes and mouth tight shut, was like that of a tiny dog, engaging rather than repulsive.

As I was conducting this examination Toffee, the ginger cat, came and sunned himself outside the shed door. When I offered the bat to him he sniffed it but showed no interest, but here's a wonder, for the first time he came to me to be petted. I put the bat on the compost heap: that's probably illegal too.

ON THE last Sunday of my duty month as I went to unlock the church a collared dove fluttered down and perched on a gravestone in the shape of a crucifix, just a few paces from me. We stared at each other, it trying first one eye then the other, before taking its time flying off. Was it trying to tell me something?

It is rather easy, quite attractive really, to surrender to mystical thoughts, especially when birds are involved – one can quite see why the Romans and others have read so much into birds' chance behaviour. Only the evening before we had been to a very powerful and moving re-enact-ment of the life of St Francis of Assisi, in words and music, in the tiny church that nestles below the ridgeway at Batcombe. It had ended, mov-ingly, with two children releasing doves from the west door.

But mysticism doesn't really work for me – at least, not for long – although I am very careful about magpies. The collared dove flew off, having seemed to have suspended time for a few moments, its wings squeaking, the way they do. Collared doves always seem to be overdue a visit to the oilcan.

Church of St Mary Magdalene, Batcombe.   I. J. Moore.

THE most alarming thing that I encountered in the church porch during my 'key worker' duties during May was my neighbour Robert, coming out of the church with a fistful of paper and a concerned face. Out of the kindness of his heart he takes care of the church fabric, and what he was holding was the architect's Quinquennial Report. He took me to the wall that separates our orchard from the graveyard.

A good 6 feet high for most of its length, it suddenly swoops up to nearly 9. Part of this tall section had taken on a perilous lean – here was something for the Poison Dwarf really to get worked up over – what was to be done about it Robert asked? I promised to do something promptly; in fact the wall gave me the heebie-jeebies, couldn't think how I had allowed such a dangerous situation to creep up unnoticed.

Through most of its great height as slender as it is tall, only two bricks thick, topped with heavy coping stones – almost cripplingly heavy, as I was to find – and well over two centuries old, it is a miracle of construction and survival. The bricks are set in forgiving mortar of course, not bound together inflexibly by cement.

The next day I set about dismantling the top three feet of the most threatening section, some four yards long. Lifting the coping stones to the ground down a ladder was quite frankly terrifying, it was so important not to drop them. Carefully shaped soft Ham stone, each a yard long, they would break easily, and be, with their patina of age, quite irreplaceable.

The first was the worst, what I call the 'swooping stone', beautifully curved, thicker than the rest, it carried the wall most of the way up to its full height. It seemed to weigh a ton, and took me down the ladder, rather than me taking it down. However, once I had got it, and its fellows, safely to the ground the rest was comparatively easy.

Except where a few patches of regrettable, later, pointing had been done in cement, the bricks could have been lifted from their 200-year-old lime-mortar beds by a child. It was filthy work, a mischievous wind blowing the dust of the old mortar into my face and eyes; I had to work down-wind, as the rams, full of curiosity and interest, made it clear that they were anxious and ready to 'help' if I were to try to work on the orchard side.

But the bricks themselves were a joy to handle. Rose-red, going on orange, mottled purple sometimes on their weather faces, with a shallow diamond shape impressed in the centre of their under-sides, they were things of beauty, to be treated with respect.

SOON the most urgent work was done, it took about two afternoons, and involved I don't know how many bricks – I tried to count them several times, and gave up. The job was now, through the summer, and before there might be any frost, which could destroy the exposed, uncapped section of the wall, to build a couple of buttresses, and somehow to struggle those massive coping stones back into place.

This is just the sort of job I relish, that, in truth, I get obsessed with, grudging every moment spent elsewhere. I would need to learn how to handle lime mortar, which I had never done before, but, apart from that, the main difficulty would be to find the time, with a myriad other summer jobs clamouring to be done. It would be a splendid foil for the glitz and glamour of the polo scene however.

But here's an odd twist that would have delighted Thomas Hardy. When it was first mooted, I had not been sure how it would take me, having my former wife's grave where I should see it almost daily. Guess where the wall overhung, most threatened to fall down – where else but just above the very spot? And, to underline the irony, as it were to rub it in, on the second day that I was working there, the undertakers came to erect her headstone.

One never knows, at least I never do, just how feelings will work. They are impenetrable, beyond any advance calculation, or much defence. When my father died, well before his time, it was as if fate had tiptoed up behind and struck me down; I still seem to think of him nearly every day. How could I do otherwise, living in a place he so left his stamp on?

But this business of the grave, though I was aware of it most of the time whilst I was working there, I found it did not trouble me – something to do with the funeral, and the family gathering on that day I think.

If I often mention Thomas Hardy do not suppose I like the man, what I think I know of him I heartily dislike, but I love his books. Our old gardener-cum-groom, Tom Dufall, long gone now, shared a birthplace with his namesake and remembered him well. "'e didn't have nothing to say to the likes o' we", Tom used to say of the creator of Marty South, Giles Winterborne and Gabriel Oak.

DANDY, short for Dandelion, the elder of our two horses, a handsome bay, and the clone of his mother Daisy, is my hunter. We have had a lot of fun together, but, truth to tell, he's a bit chicken where I need a lion. His predecessor, Woody, would carry me anywhere, his pace would quicken as soon as he saw jump, you barely had to ask him. But Woody is now living in extreme old age on a horse farm in the Bicester country, along with his stablemate, Diana's old hunter The Bean. They give blood monthly, but otherwise live a life of ease and sociability – near enough heaven on earth for horses I suppose and hope.

But Dandy is the horse I've got. I am very fond of him; as far as age goes we are on converging trajectories, he fourteen, I past seventy, we should just about see each other out. I don't, can't think of ever parting with, or replacing him. One sunny morning we set out together to attempt to retrace the line of 'The Old Sherborne Road', where it used to pass just by this village, but is now lost entirely in the fields.

In a light-hearted, light-headed moment a year before I had offered to conduct the annual Village Outing, and now, suddenly, a date was fixed, and the cloud that had been no larger than a man's hand threatened to blot out the sun. I had to get down to working out how I was going to interest my neighbours in what so interests me, the line of what I call our 'Ghost Road'.

Our annual Outing, is not, as you may have supposed, an occasion to bring joy and happiness to the hearts all those Gender Diversity Outreach Co-ordinators who play such a vital role in rural life, it is a fund-raising tractor ride and supper, run for the benefit of our Village Hall.

It has become immensely popular, attracts people from all round; well over a hundred of us, of all ages, sitting on straw bales on long trailers drawn by half-a-dozen or more tractors, are taken round a bit of the parish that has some history attached – someone gives a talk about it. This year, as you have gathered, that someone is to be me.

SO OFF Dandy and I set, out of the village, up Stock Hill, past the Manor, and over to Round Chimneys, now a farm, but once the seat of the Churchill family and the boyhood home of the 1st Duke of Marlborough. Soon the lane broadened out into an old cattle drove, and we got to the spot where one of the several roads that through the Middle Ages used to connect Sherborne with Dorchester once crossed it, but where today is just a T-junction*.

Here our adventure and struggles were due to start. I had of course obtained the owner's permission, readily given, to ride across his land. The first gate was a real fight. It was in a boundary hedge of course, overgrown with rampant briar and little used – why hadn't I brought secateurs? But Dandy enjoyed grazing the lush grass at the length of his reins whilst I forced the gate open and shut, occasionally jerking my hands off their work as he stretched for the next inviting tussock.

One long narrow field, telling you as clear as a field sometimes can that it once carried an old road, brought us to the next challenge, an electric fence, which might or might not be live – why hadn't I asked Brian about his electric fencing?

Dandy knows very well what electric fences are, and they bring out the whirling dervish in him: so I had to lay the wire flat with him now a fighting salmon at the length of his reins. However he came over stepping soberly enough where I had laid my jacket on it – we had done this often enough before, he knew the drill – and had recovered his equanimity sufficiently to allow him to graze contentedly again whilst I re-erected it.

Soon we were onto the regular track leading from pasture to farmyard, the hum of Brian's milking machine was in my ears, and the first part of the 'recce', enough for one morning, was successfully done. I wondered, as I rode the short distance home, who was the very last person to ride that stretch of road, and when. It fell into disuse, became a ghost, when speed and wheels became all-important, and the A 352 was first surfaced for stage-coaches, then given a tarmac coating for the motorcar.

I also fell to wondering if I would have the bottle to conduct the Outing on horseback – we shall see.

More about the Old Sherborne Road, and a map, are to be found at the back of the book in the Appendix.

JUNE

THERE can be few better places or occasions to enjoy and revel in the 'forces of conservatism' – such a useful phrase, thank you Mr Blair – than the Royal Bath and West Show.

We were lucky enough to be guests of the Chairman, and I had read his Report in the show's Annual Review with considerable interest and respect. He had written of the farmer being "virtually a prisoner of bureaucracy", of how "a great industry found itself alienated on its own turf, and (that) the established practices and customs of the country were being challenged and controlled by townspeople".

He went on to lament "the long running saga of the campaign against field sports in general and hunting in particular.... with... all the worst elements of government based on envy or prejudice... paraded... by the media". "A blade of cold steel has pierced the heart of every countryman in the land" he said. But that day at Shepton Mallet, rather like one of our

London Marches, was the perfect antidote to Brown-study and Blair-gloom – with cattle, horses, farming folk galore, and a strong dash of the military, past and present.

Whether it was a magnificent Tamworth sow with here litter, the Show's 'Village Green' with its bandstand, church, school, village hall and ringing smithy, or the bands in the arena that most impressed me, I don't know. But I hope that I shall never forget the pipes and dancers of that magnificent regiment the Black Watch (there's a 'force of conservatism' for you), or the sudden irruption into the arena of sixteen Household cavalry troopers on their blacks for a musical ride.

When the two roughriders, or 'monkeys' as they are called, on a drum beat, made their mounts lie down, it was a pleasure to see those canny blacks snatch the odd blade of arena grass in the side of their mouths when they were meant to be acting dead.

It had indeed been a day for the child in all of us, but in many ways also a strengthening and reassuring day for one who fears for farming, hates to see it shrinking, threatened. Political sophisticates may reason away this island's need to feed itself, but I can't see it. You cannot eat CD's, DVD's and floppy discs: let's hope we never have to try to.

"WON'T you find that stick a bit of a nuisance?" Diana asked next morning as I put my shepherd's crook into the boot of the car. I was off to London again, this time not only sure of seeing the Westminster Retable, but feeling quite self-important. I had been summoned by an Editor to discuss how we hunting correspondents were going to be able to continue to earn a crust next season without putting our friends in gaol, or ourselves ending up behind bars.

Instead of blundering around blindly beneath London, I had decided this time to stay above ground – I never walk anywhere without a favourite thumbstick or my crook if I can help it. A Welsh ram's horn mounted on hazel, it is a souvenir of a hunting expedition in Snowdonia given me by our late rector: I treasure it.

Getting away had been something of a rush. Dandy was still fast asleep, with Bella standing beside him, when I went to fetch them into the paddock, both of course at the very far end of our five acres. He gave a deep groan when I slipped his head-collar over his ears, thought about rolling, thought better of it, then staggered up in that peculiarly incompetent and dangerous way horses have of struggling to their feet – you would think that it was the first time they had ever done it – me standing off at the full length of the rope. I remember all too well what it is like being amongst those mailed milling feet.

London this time answered hope and disappointed fear. The meeting was good value, I walked the best part of five miles, and the Retable was memorable. The National Gallery struck me as something really to be proud of, the collection so magnificently displayed, the staff so courteous. When I asked at the reception desk if I should deposit my shepherd's crook the reply came "if you need your stick Sir, by all means take it in with you": this proved too great a test of both my honesty and my pride, I hung onto it.

JUST AS many who go hunting do so for the sake of the ride, and, contrary-wise, many go to point-to-points for anything but to watch the racing, so, I am convinced, a majority of those who attend puppy shows are thinking of nothing but the tea. It is natural enough, puppy shows are splendid occasions, but are very specialised in their interest, very recondite, dwelling as they do, sometimes at agonising length, on the minute differences in hounds that are, to many of those present, almost identical.

Puppy shows are also splendidly English. One dresses up, ignores the weather, so often arctic in June, and feigns a close interest in what is going on, not least so that that demigod, the Huntsman, may be persuaded one is appreciative, knowledgeable and keen. As a hunting correspondent, I have a special interest in being mistaken for an expert, and work hard at it.

Of all the puppy shows in the land, I cannot believe that that there is a finer one than that of the Cattistock Hunt, or a tea that is more worth waiting and risking hypothermia for. The hounds are shown in the great stable yard at Melbury House. Because this is a strange and intimidating setting for the puppies, who look older than they are, and, like a bumptious child suddenly rendered dumb by appearing in front of an audience at her school play, can be overwhelmed by the occasion, a rehearsal is held the week before. Since at the time I was writing something about hound puppies, I was lucky enough to be invited to this rather private occasion.

Driving up to the house from the lodge in Evershot could have been designed, no doubt was so designed, to put the likes of me in my place – the approach is awe-inspiring. Had I not known the *châtelaine* to be a person of exemplary kindness and approachability, I might have turned and run; just as a young bitch called Christmas was to do in the judging ring a week later. I am not at my happiest, solo, on such occasions.

I should have known better. I found myself among friends, just a handful of cognoscenti who had turned out to see the young entry looked over by a couple of professional huntsmen – both great men in their world, and in mine, Tony Wright from the Exmoor, and Chris Bowld of the Blackmore & Sparkford Vale. (All were informally dressed for this holiday occasion, but why was Tony wearing a National Trust tie, he must loathe the National Trust? Perhaps it was in conscious irony, I didn't dare to ask him.)

Afterwards, typically, we were all asked into the house for a drink, and were entertained in the billiard-room, an extraordinarily cavernous, tall and intimidating chamber which, in the evening light, seemed to have no ceiling, and was hung, several deep, with ancestral portraits, each one the size of the wall of a small room. Our hostess handed round delicious 'eats', as though to members of her own family.

Far from being daunting, it had turned into a very happy occasion. The setting, in that great Ham stone yard, was memorable. The ghostly face of a grey horse, absent a week later, had watched the rehearsal throughout, looking very intelligent and interested, over a stable half-door. And a blackbird carolled away on the chimneys and roof pinnacles of the house.

But what I can't forget was the blue tit that had seemed to dive across my path straight through a shut stable door, as I had made my way from my car on arriving – it was like conjuring trick. The door, which evidently was out of use, had one of those old-fashioned flush latches that you lift by pressing a button – specially designed, as all good stable furniture is, so that no passing rein or stirrup leather could catch on it.

The latch-button was missing, leaving a florin-sized hole, and the little bird had dived, without a check, straight through. If it were me, I would certainly fail to fold my wings in time, or would infallibly catch my beak and spill its precious load, but this little ace had perfect timing and the precise trajectory; it was like a fragment of film run backwards. A split-second, and I would have missed it, but it was memory to carry home, a tiny miracle of nature. As William Blake has it, 'a world in a grain of sand'.

DIANA came with me on the day of the Puppy Show itself. The great yard was crowded and alive, the ring surrounded on three sides by chairs, and on the fourth by an agricultural trailer mounted with straw bales for children to watch from. This, either intentionally or not, provided an alternative attraction for the straying eye. Soon a straw-fight was in progress, girls versus boys, the girls getting the best of it, as far as I could tell... when I could spare a glance from the all-important proceedings in the ring.

Puppy shows follow an immutable and all but sacred formula. First the young dog hounds, a couple at a time, are brought into the ring, the huntsman loudly naming them, and with judicious biscuits, showing them off to the two bowler-hatted judges. Then all the dog hounds are brought in together, and the weeding-out begins.

It's the exact opposite to that schooldays ordeal when you wait to be picked, or in my case not picked, for a team. Out of the corner of his mouth, usually the junior of the two judges, names or indicates a reject, the huntsman calls its name, and it is expelled, dragged by the scruff or carried, in ignominy, whence it came.

When just two couple are left they are taken and put through their paces, in the open, somewhere handy. This is the first major test of the spectator's keenness: the correct thing to do is leave your seat and press forward eagerly, in order not to miss one single second of the judging. Some people, I regret to say, just keep their seats and chat.

On return, the order of merit is announced: in my experience the winner is usually the palest coloured hound. Lay people generally prefer dark coloured hounds, experts know better: if you doubt my theory, test it at the next puppy show you got to.

The judging of the bitches, always more numerous, follows. Next, the winning dog and bitch are shown together, the overall champion announced, prizes are handed out to the well-deserving puppy walkers, speeches are made, and we break up for tea.

And, at Melbury, what a tea it always is. The great thing is to get into the Library early – not just so as to have a first go at all the good things on offer, there surely never was such a spread, but also to see that enormous room laid out to receive its guests, and to get a clear view of the life-size almost, group equine portrait at the far end. Soon it's chatter, chatter, chatter of a hundred friends and more, and, for many, the serious business of another hunt puppy show is under way.

ONE thing that I noticed in my two happy visits to Melbury made me, and may make you smile. I took careful note of the order in which hounds were rejected on each occasion, and which hounds eventually took the prizes. There was absolutely no co-relation between the decisions of the judges at the rehearsal and on the actual day: for instance, the winning dog hound at the rehearsal was the first to be rejected by the judges a week later.

It is so easy to be clever when you are just watching, a truism that applies especially to those of my trade. What I learned from this disparity, something I already partly knew, is that judging hounds, judging anything in that line I guess, is a subjective business. There are no absolutes, huntsmen know what they look for in a hound, and no two huntsmen look for exactly the same thing.

OUR Church Fête this year fell on the same day as the Queen's official birthday, so there was a double reason for the St George's cross to be flying from the tower flagpole, a sight I always relish. But the bunting, hundreds of small union jacks strung up this way and that over the churchyard, all silvery in the low morning sun, caught Dandy's eye as I led him and his sister first thing across the lane to the paddock.

He stood for a moment rigid, on tiptoe, full height, at once magnificent and rather frightening. I didn't know quite what he had in mind to do next, immediate flight was clearly a possibility. But the moment passed, and just as well, the morning of the fête is no time for diversions: the field has to be turned into a car park, and there were a dozen other things to be done.

As I had been recently reminded in my work on the church wall, the first principle of all outdoor work is that 'one thing leads to another', and the second that 'the implement you most need is the one you left on the bench in the shed'. Thus, as I put out the parking signs I noticed the heaps of dung dotted here and there that, for the honour of the house as well as the enrichment of the compost heap, needed to be removed. In shifting them my eye lighted on the thistles, I fetched the scythe... and so on.

All village fêtes are much the same: I won't bore you with the details. Suffice it to say that my eldest son and his wife Anna, she expecting their first child, were staying with us. Charlie, who has a master's degree in such things, is a computer wizard, Anna is a doctor, specialising in Public Health, they live in Leamington. As well as being the Queen's, it was Charlie's, fortieth, birthday; we celebrated with a single candle in a slice of cake bought at the fête tea. It was a very happy, sunny day.

WHEN the three R's and Blunkett returned from being shorn they brought a fifth ram with them. I initially named him Ishmael, because the others seemed to shun him, and he is always on his own. The other rams are all as plump as plump, but he, poor thing, is painfully thin, skeletal in fact, I guess rather old, and missing his fur coat in this unseasonable weather. He seems to want to attach himself to me, to flatter me with close attendance, is always on the lookout, and gives a baa of recognition when he sees me

Whenever, needs must, I was working with my hawk and trowel on the orchard side of the wall he will come and stand just behind me, his old box-shaped head lifted, cocked on one side inquiringly – had I perhaps some little thing for him to eat he seems to ask, would I at least just scratch his face?

When I scythed the nettles recently he came and paddled in them, finding and gratefully gobbling up the cow parsley and other good things that had hitherto been un-get-at-able. And when I pick the strawberries, he is there to eat any rejects, or the weeds that I throw over the hurdles to him.

Sometimes when I go to check on him I find him, combining Old Testament with New, taking his ease beneath our Judas tree. This has driven me to the Good Book, to be reminded that Ishmael "was a wild man; his hand … turned against every man, and every man's hand turned against him", also that he was cast out, ostracised, because he was the Abraham family *au pair's* lovechild, which seems less than fair. I concluded that the name Ishmael didn't fit and wouldn't do.

Since, when he isn't lying down, he often stands with his head drooping, looking mournful and dejected, I have decided that a better name for him is Eeyore. Sheep never miss a chance of dying: I've a nasty feeling that Eeyore is not long for this world. I hope I am wrong, quite a strong mutual attachment seems to have grown up between us.

STAIR-RODS, freezing cold, and it's exactly the middle of June. Last Sunday I was huddled in a Barbour on the stands at Smith's Lawn, what chance of a spot of sunshine for next Saturday's big match at Westonbirt? Where is summer, there's not a sign of any dry, settled weather yet, just growing weather for the wretched grass, which is for ever getting out of hand?

My first thought on getting up was for Eeyore. An upstairs window showed some of the rams huddled under the small shelter that I built years ago for our own lambs, under a buttress in the orchard. I bet myself Eeyore was, as usual, in Coventry. But in fact, when I got out there, I found that he had secured inside position in the shelter, against the wall.

He stood, head drooped in the buttress angle, wheel-backed and hunched. I don't like the look of him one little bit, but what can one do – all his wives and offspring are far worse off, out in the open fields – nature will just have to take its course? And I daren't tell Diana, she won't sleep a wink if I do.

We had planned a ride through Hay Wood to the egg farm, but the weather forecast had said "Wait!". I had decided that the horses themselves should tell me whether they wanted to stay in the meadow, with its shelter, or to come across as usual to the lush grass in the paddock for the day.

They were in what we call the corral, the enclosure with its shelter just inside the gate, contentedly grazing. They looked up, then went on grazing, looked up again – I decided that if they came towards me I'd get the head-collars and fetch them across – but, no, they seemed to be happy where they were, so I left them.

You could see no more that a veiled suggestion of the Heights, still shrouded in low cloud and rain. Who knows, we might get the eggs this afternoon… meanwhile there was yesterday's brickwork to be inspected; at least the weather was ideal for slow-setting lime mortar?

"OH GOD, the strawberries!" I say to myself as they catch my eye when, having dealt with the horses, I pay a quick visit to Eeyore before settling down to a busy day in which every minute seems to be mortgaged. The kitchen garden can be such a bully sometimes; the strawberries won't be denied.

On the previous evening, when we got back from the polo at Beaufort, after a long drive in a sudden heat wave and with an article buzzing around trying to get out of my head, the last thing one wanted… there was evidently more trouble with the rams. Blunkett was walking round in small circles looking lost, in the paddock, when he ought by rights to be in the orchard.

A quick inspection revealed that he had carried away half a rood of sheep wire, leaving a body-print in it that I am sure would win a Turner prize. He then had blundered straight on through the hedge that Jasper and I so carefully cut-and-laid two Christmases ago, into the church lane, whence, evidently, some kind neighbour had turned him into the paddock. We should soon hear no doubt who did this good deed; but what had so maddened him, driven him, that is usually so placid, to such extremes, was a mystery. Perhaps we should have guessed.

I had not quite appreciated just how sightless poor Blunkett was until I tried to get him back to the orchard. He kept darting, blind, in this direction or that, crashing into whatever might be in his path, a tree, or the paddock railings. It was horrible to witness, for the damage he might do to himself; he already had blood all over his face from his previous exploits.

In the end I found that, if I arrested him, with a hand under his neck and one behind his tail, and talked to him gently, he came quietly enough. This way I propelled him across the lawn back to where he belonged. He's rather a dear really, and the others seemed really glad to see him.

WE were not left guessing long about the cause of Blunkett's rampage. A few mornings later, first thing, frantic barking in the orchard revealed a Jack Russell terrier bating him, his poor face streaming blood from crashing into the apple trees in a horrid game of blind man's buff.

What to do? First the terrier had to be pursued home and told on. Then Blunkett's wounds bathed and cleaned with saline, for which he stood docile, endearingly trustful and patient. There were two long ugly gashes, one close by his eye, one by his mouth and nostril – they looked worse than they were... I hoped. I manoeuvred him to join his companions who were cowering, keeping close company, out of sight behind a wall.

Then came what was potentially by far the trickiest part, something had to be done about the dog, and done without causing bad blood to flow – dogs can be as difficult as drains and ditches when they become an issue between neighbours. Fortunately good sense prevailed.

By the way, Eeyore has gone – I forgot to tell you. 'Gone' in the literal rather than the tragic sense. Despite my sly discretion, Diana cottoned on to my worries about his state of health, rang Neil, who has taken him away. The last I saw of him his great head was thrust between the bars of Neil's trailer, he seemed to be looking pleadingly at me, and not to want to go.

JULY

I WAS in the kitchen when Melanie, our eldest, Jasper's mother, rang – "There are bombs going off in London, did you know?". I had hardly put the telephone on its rest before Louise rang from Milan, "Are Melanie and Jasper safe; where's Mum?". Like, I guess, families all over the country, we were checking up on the people who come first in our minds – the girls were lucky to get through, and I was so grateful to have the right answer ready for Louise when she rang. Mel had been on the way to a hair appointment, and had turned back, Jasper was in good hands.

Whatever horrors follow, who can forget that first moment of realization that the war had spread to this country, we were at last under direct attack? Diana was out, I couldn't leave the house until I knew how much she knew, and should be able to answer her immediate question.

I didn't anyway care to leave the wireless, so I hung around, looking out into the kitchen yard; a view normally enjoyed by the back of my head as I sit in the window seat. That small rectangular courtyard is a rather lovely feature of the place, surrounded on three sides by the house and its outbuildings, with a coalhouse and open log-shelter framing a small gateway at the far end.

Diana keeps it full of flowers, and, with no Perdita to maintain order, it has become something of a wildlife park. A tiny frog has taken up residence under the bench, among the wellies in the porch on the right. Flycatchers nest in the log-shelter at the far end, also wagtails, if the flycatchers will let them, and, if there are enough logs left over from winter, wrens.

The Flycatchers were busy feeding their brood as I watched, in and out every few seconds – their young must have been nearly ready for take-off – swallows and a pair of greenfinches swooped in and out of view, a handsome cock-blackbird was jumping up and down off the paving like a basketball player, not scoring goals but pinching berries off the honeysuckle on the coalhouse wall.

As I watched, a baby rabbit came hip-hop in through the gateway to nibble the weeds that will grow in the cracks in the floor of the shelter. And then a moment of drama – if it had been an opera the orchestra would have struck a sonorous minor chord – Toffee, the gamekeeper's gate, stalked in. I saw the fierce switch of his tail over the greenery as he pounced. Exit Toffee with another baby rabbit in his jaws.

All this, whilst broadcasters were describing the developing scene in London: it was difficult to leave the house that day. For once one felt grateful to the officials who told us in a straightforward way what was going on, and reasonably proud of the politicians who spoke for us. They expressed themselves simply, naturally, and with dignity. There was no gushing clichés about "my heart going out" as if the speaker were a cuckoo clock its heart popping out of a little door on a spring; or "remembering in our prayers" by people one could not possibly imagine on their knees.

THERE were seven tractors and trailers parked in a line in the small meadow behind the Village Hall a week later on the evening of the Outing, and over two hundred tickets sold. I had got the scale of the thing entirely wrong, had imagined myself talking intimately to a handful of fascinated neighbours. I had actually selected which tussock I was going to stand on at each stopping place, and endlessly assured Diana that I would "Speak up!", not mumble.

Paul, the organizer, had come round that morning with the bad news that the thing was a howling success, a fine evening was forecast, everyone would turn up, and that, willy-nilly, I was, for the first time in my life, to use that loathed thing, a PA system. The rest of the day was torment, the early evening, as I sat on a hay bale on the leading tumbrel, torture. I just longed for it all to be over, longed even more for a drink, several drinks.

I expect you think that I am going to tell you that after all it was a great triumph. Well it wasn't. From my point of view it was a fiasco. I didn't get half the things I wanted to say, said. Even with the wretched microphone, which I couldn't get the hang of and was death to any sort of rapport, I was drowned out half the time by the whooping and shouting of myriad children, who, of course, didn't give a pin for the Old Sherborne Road.

It's an old story. Owlish, earnest me, totally disconnecting with the frivolous world… and being forgiven for it; every one was very kind. I decided to stay dumb at the final stand on Loader's Hill (see map with the Appendix), whilst the children spilt down the sunlit slope like quicksilver, in all directions. It was a heavenly evening, and such a treat to see the village and Dungeon Hill from that viewpoint, a pastoral symphony really.

IT'S impossible to pass through Salisbury, either by road or train, without being overcome anew by wonder at its cathedral spire.

Driving up from Blandford, dropping off the high down, the road is suddenly swallowed by a magnificent winding coombe that always seems an impressive overture to what follows. Then, shortly, "Wow!", 'the finger of God' is in front of you. Is there anything, anywhere, anywhere in the world indeed, to match it? How on earth did the bare unaided hands of man contrive to raise and shape such a mass of stone so high, so beautifully?

What wonder, what architect's dream of our so clever modern world touches that spire for audacity and grace? As William Cobbett wrote when one of his *Rural Rides* took him through Salisbury in 1826, "Such a thing could never be made *now*". Truly it is a sermon in stone, and it puts twentyfirst century man in his place.

It was, also, a rather admonitory 'finger' as we passed it on the Sunday morning following the Village Outing, on the way to Cowdray for the Gold Cup. But it was a welcoming sight as it came into view again as we passed below Figsbury Ring on the Roman Road coming home.

By a strange freak it was just at that moment that the car wireless told us of a venerable statesman being on his deathbed in the Cathedral Close below us. Personalities apart, the death of a Prime Minister is surely a moment to ponder, it demeans the State if we do not respect that office.

But what is one to make of the announcer who chose to say that Sir Edward Heath "ruled the country for four years"?

How does one survive schooling in this country, achieve adulthood, and get appointed to an important post in the BBC, believing that our Prime Minister 'rules' us? And was there no-one supervising and correcting the ignorant maunderings of this harpy that she repeated the howler an hour later? Perhaps she is paid to flatter the fantasies of the present incumbent of 10 Downing Street, who, I seem to remember, referred in a recent Christmas broadcast to "my armed forces"?

Happier thoughts brought Anthony Trollope to mind, and the opening chapter of *Barchester Towers*, when, in the author's imagination, the old bishop lay dying in that same Close. His son, Archdeacon Grantly, and his old friend, Septimus Harding, depicted at the dying bishop's bedside, are two of the most sympathetically drawn characters in English literature.

The character of the Archdeacon is another admonitory finger, even if it is raised by Trollope in the kindest possible way. I'm sure that we all have a bit of that proud, harsh man in us, I know that I do; and who does not try to be as lamblike as Warden Harding? I'm truly sorry for my uncharitable reference to the maunderings of that harpy at the BBC, and my imputation of delusions of grandeur in 10 Downing Street.

THERE has been positive blizzard of 'stiffies' this summer, the cork board in the kitchen is snowed over with pasteboard, invitations galore, a high proportion of which bespeak not only the pleasure of our company but the contents of our wallets. It is proving a very expensive season, and it kicked off with a truly splendid event in aid of Salisbury Cathedral, at Melbury.

A high proportion of fund-raising seems to be for parish churches. Most PCCs no doubt struggle, as we in Glanvilles Wootton do, to meet the annual 'quota' needed to support that other, less edifying, edifice, the Salisbury diocesan funds. What ever did the Church do with all the contents of its once swelling coffers?

Quite the happiest such evening was spent in a marquee on the green in the tiny village of Hermitage, not 5 miles from here. It was called Opera Soufflé, the 'Darling Divas' were to perform, "Bring your own picnic... Tickets £12.50 each!".

Darling Divas indeed, there were two of them, singing and acting arias and cabaret to a very clever accompaniment on an electronic keyboard. One of the singers suddenly fastened her eyes on me, advanced, and sat on my lap, made out I was her unfaithful boyfriend, whilst her companion claimed to be engaged to be married to me.

How often, past three-score years and ten, does one get fought over by pretty girls? I can't remember a more enjoyable evening, where I have laughed more or longer, or got better value for a pony; Diana enjoyed it too.

In the picnic interval, quite out of the blue, our old regimental padre suddenly materialised. He came with us to Ulster, we thought the world of him, and he has recently retired to live nearby. "Up to your old tricks still I see!" he said, wagging yet another reproving finger.

SUMMER dinner parties cast an especially long shadow. Not only is much of the house uninhabitable, one's presence unwelcome unless peremptorily demanded, to hold this, or carry that, but everything outside, so helpfully invisible in winter, must be made spic and span. You can imagine therefore that I was not best pleased to be met by Blunkett blundering around in the drive, as I was nipping off on Bella for a quick spin over the hill before devoting the day to singeing the garden's whiskers.

There was nothing for it but to put a puzzled and belligerent Bella back in her box, rope Blunkett, and bundle him back whence he came – I have become quite expert at this. How he escaped from the well-fenced paddock is a mystery. Back in the saddle, I fully expected as I rode down the hedge beside the drive, to find it breeched, but no such thing.

On return I walked every inch of the fencing – there was nothing to show of a violent escape. Nor was there any trace on his poor old face of any damage from crashing into things, as there had been when he was worried by the neighbour's terrier in the orchard. Somehow, he had levitated himself over the iron railings, goodness knows how or where, there was no trace of wool on them.

When I put him back with the others, it was rather touching to see how they welcomed him. I never thought that I would use the word, but they seem to be 'caring'. He immediately lay down amongst them – he must have been out on the loose all night. He had certainly wrecked my day, which had now to include getting the rams onto fresh ground, lest we have Blunkett gate crashing the dinner party, joining us for champagne and canapés on the manicured lawn.

ALL you will wish to know about the dinner party is that, despite my begging them not to rush off so soon, the first guests to leave did so at 1am. If I add that the burglar alarm cried "Wolf!" twice during what was left of the night, you can perhaps imagine what sort of shape the master of the house was in next morning.

The rams, who had run snuffling, gobbling and grunting with greedy delight when I moved them into the larger of our two paddocks, soon got fed up with it, and showed clear sign of wanting to be somewhere, any-where, else. They clustered in a miserable group round the gate, when-ever they weren't stuffing themselves with the plentiful grass, catching my eye and making me feel guilty.

When Sunday dawned, a full, wet gale blowing, and we needed to get on the road to Windsor for Cartier International Day, the high point of the polo season, one of the rams was missing. It was one of the three Rs, not Blunkett this time. I was already soaked through my Barbour, from visiting the horses, but there was nothing for it but to take a run round looking for the deserter, warn the neighbours, ring Neil, the owner of the rams.

Just as we were leaving Lyn, who looks after the horses at Church Farm, trotted up the drive on their little Arab. There was a ram on his own, and looking quite contented, in Stonylongs, she reported. Panic over, off we set for a day rubbing shoulders with 'celebrities', and, as it hap-pened, to watch one of the best Coronation Cup matches I have seen in years.

AUGUST

ON A still day, or better, if there is a light wind from the west, and if there are no tractors growling around, one sometimes hears a train rattle up the single-track railway that runs from Weymouth up to Bath, Bristol and beyond. About once a year, as we did yesterday, we catch it at Yetminster, barely 6 miles away – you have to flag it down, like a bus – to go to a matinée in Jane Austen's Theatre Royal at Bath.

It's a risky business going to the theatre as seldom as we do. Ten-to-one some super-clever Director will have indulged himself in some freak, and spoiled your treat, by setting *A Midsummer-Night's Dream* in an igloo, casting an albino as Othello, or staging costume drama in the nude, all performed in front of ugly minimalist scenery.

But we were in luck. Peter Hall had done nothing more outrageous than to ask us to imagine that *Much Ado About Nothing* took place at the time the theatre first opened, exactly 200 years ago. Hero and Beatrice were dressed as Jane would have been dressed at that time, and their lovers were in the gorgeous soldiers' uniforms of that day. It was blissful, and we were in the company of good friends.

I HAD been disgusted by the noise and teeming sordid bustle of the Bath streets. Before the theatre, whilst Diana was buying a very fetching velvet jacket in Gap, once I had done my duty of approving it, I fled the airless shop and waited in what passes in a city for fresh air. A burglar alarm was constantly ringing, unheeded, the pavement was a scrum, the whole thing my idea of hell.

Seen from the train on the journey home the contrast of the healing grandeur of the empty farmland was striking. For mile on mile one might not see a house, and then, as you cross the Sparkford Vale, there is suddenly Cadbury Castle, with its suggestions of history and legend, and the almost savage skyline behind it.

The notion of empty space in the countryside is of course an illusion, there are eyes everywhere, nothing goes unnoticed. When I was riding Bella next morning, the imp that always sits on my shoulder whispered "The hay has just been taken off this field, why not go for a gallop round it? It would do no harm: no-one will know."

I shan't tell you exactly where we were, but it was a field surrounded almost by woodland. We had barely completed half our guilty circuit off the public path before a dog barked and I saw two people, and saw that they saw me. I made sure of meeting up with them where our ways converged at the gate into the wood, confessed my sin, established that they were neutral parties, and went on my way, sobered, a reformed character... until the next time.

MY FATHER is seldom fresher in my memory than when I am holding his Shakespeare. Printed on rice paper by the Oxford University Press in the 1920s, although it has well over a thousand pages it is no bulkier than the average novel. He must have bought it, no doubt at Blackwell's, when he was 'up', at New College. It travelled with him round the world in the war, was much read, the binding is almost in tatters. Following our Bath trip I have just been repairing it.

He was a deeply serious, studious man, believing that, to adapt a modern phrase, you are what you read, hear and see, particularly what you read. As children we were not allowed comics, or 'comic papers' as

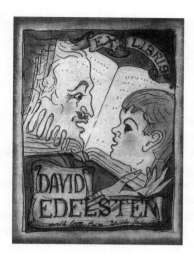

he insisted that we call them – he loathed cheap vulgarity of any sort – and there was no TV set in this house before his death.

When he was home on one of his brief leaves in the war we listened to ITMA together, we all found Tommy Handley and his crew terrific fun. It must have been a repeat broadcast we were listening to one time, as I had told him that I loved the song – the programme always had a musical interlude in it – he listened to it expressionless, and said that he didn't find it the least bit amusing, and couldn't imagine why I did.

By the same token, when, completely lost as to what profession I was to follow, I went on a school careers visit to British American Tobacco in Avon Docks, and told him that it had looked an interesting line to follow, he replied "I suppose so... if you don't mind completely wasting your life".

Yet he was the gentlest of men, I seldom heard him raise his voice, never saw him hurry. He just had the highest of high standards, took endless pains, something his patients, who adored him, certainly never complained about.

When he occasionally came home from the war it was a great excitement to watch him unpack his trunk, and to see what presents he had brought for us children – things usually that he had made in the long empty hours at sea. He spent most of the war afloat.

One time he brought back for me a slim blue book, a Penguin, that he had bound himself. Having never bound a book before, he had managed the thing somehow in the cramped privacy of his cabin, using whatever materials he could find. Like everything he turned his hand to, it was a miracle of skill, patience... and love.

Inside the cover, in a bookplate, the ghost of the Bard is talking to a wrapt small boy, recognisably me, before an open folio. The book itself is Hesketh Pearson's *Life of Shakespeare*, a strange present for an eleven-year-old boy, but don't I just appreciate it, and the giver, now?

As I got older I could actually help him with whatever project he had in hand. The door through the orchard wall into the churchyard is a typical piece of his handiwork. A double layer of oak planks laid across each other is held together by nails driven through, and turned down on the reverse side.

We hand-forged the latch and so on, but the nails are a bit of a cheat; we didn't make them, we just brought them to red-heat and wrought the heads a bit, all two hundred of them, so that they lost their factory-made look, then painted them. He was a perfectionist, was my father.

If the man I have tried to describe comes across as cold, distant and a bit of a prig, he was none of these things. Certainly he belonged to the old school of parent that would send shivers down the spine of a modern cuddle-gush life-style guru – I cannot remember him ever embracing me. Perhaps our most intimate moment of that sort was when he asked me to shave him, the last time I was with him, when he was dying. I worshiped him: I still do.

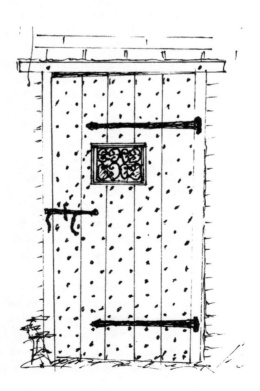

I SHIELDED my face as I left the Beauty Centre in Swan Yard – sent there to buy nail varnish, it wouldn't do to have been mistaken for a client. I was in Sherborne, on the excuse of a dentist's appointment, but really to spend an idle, congenial second half of the morning, coffee-housing, by which I mean reading the paper, and mooching around.

It was a Monday, the first day of August. I had done my polo write-up from the previous day, we'd ridden the horses, and I just wanted the rest of the morning to take charge of itself, somehow get me through to lunchtime – I needed to unwind, to do the most difficult thing in the world, to relax.

As I was leaving home an arresting scene had made me stop the car at the head of the drive. The rams were having a stand-off with Sooty, the tom cat, straining their great heads through the paddock railings at him: he staring back at them. As far as I could judge, Sooty was pondering what his dignity required of him to do next.

Then a diversion occurred. Toffee, the gamekeeper's ginger cat entered stage left. One of the rams turned and charged him, he nipped through the railings to safety.

Next it was the turn of the two cats to sort out who was boss – I had never seen them together before. At first Sooty affected not to notice the other, but Toffee crouched, swished his tail, made as if to attack. The old warrior calmly sat down, appeared to say something, which I couldn't hear over the car engine, and stared at him.

After what seemed an age – I'd never make a proper naturalist – Toffee suddenly recollected an appointment elsewhere, Sooty indulged in a self satisfied roll on the gravel… and I remembered the dentist.

ALL of the above was witnessed by a particularly dim rabbit that lives in the paddock. At least I think it's dim, Diana says it isn't well – she has displaced hypochondria, seldom fancying herself sick, she is very quick to think animals unwell, and is full of compassion for them. Anyway, this rabbit appears to mistake me for a horse, leastways it pays no attention when I am leading the horses in off grass, crouches a couple of feet from me, doesn't budge an inch.

Dandy however takes considerable notice of the rams as I lead him and Bella through the paddock. I presume that he finds their rather obvious masculinity a challenge, if not a personal insult. He makes as if to take a run at them as they reluctantly get to their feet and shuffle out of the gateway at our approach. I don't doubt, and experience suggests, that he would give them a hard time if were to try to graze them together.

Dungeon had been lovely that morning – perfect view all round, from the west edge of Salisbury Plain almost to Exmoor. Something had disturbed my neighbour's ewes up on Whitedown, the field that crowns the hill. They were all in a huddle, like a deputation, with one of their number at their head seeming to be approaching us with a petition or complaint. There was no sign of what had troubled them.

In Stonylongs, almost home, a pair of roe got up in front of us. Siblings of last year's breeding, and not quite players in the adult world, they will be looking for new living-quarters, having recently been told to get lost by their mother who suddenly has next year's brood in mind. Their lovely toast-coloured flanks reflected the sun as they fled. And, as we got onto our own ground, a single, large, black bird flew, purposefully, straight, from horizon to horizon, high overhead, croaking. Was it a raven?

BEFORE riding, and after writing, and getting my 'copy' away by the magic of e-mail, whilst waiting for Diana and the horses to have their breakfast, I had listened to some music… and I mean listened. I had actually forced myself to concentrate on every bar of Elgar's cello concerto, the heart-breaking du Pré, Barbirolli recording. It is almost too much if you are feeling at all blue, but perfect if you just want to bring your mind back from wherever it has got to, ferreting around after words that will play hide-and-seek in the roof-spaces of one's memory.

Bella was her usual saucy self when I tacked her up. *"Che faccia!"* I say to her, practising my Italian – we are due out in Santa Marguerita again at the end of the month – "What a face!". And *"Non dammi quello squardo di ragazzaccia"*, "Don't give me that grumpy teen-age look" – such useful phrases.

The horses have become sugar addicts recently. Usually I spoil them with specially designed sweets, called 'herbals', which, like Matron used to at my preparatory school, I keep in a jar, on a shelf in the saddle room. They make their breath smell particularly pleasant; not that horses ever suffer from bad breath, that being one of the many advantages that they have over humans.

But I ran out of herbals one time recently, and bought a box of Tate & Lyle cubes – they adore them, search all my pockets for them. Now they are gone, but, when there was only one left, guess who got it? Not deserving, useful, dutiful Dandy of course, but his adorable scatty sister.

THAT evening I planted out the last of my leeks. One shouldn't have favourites, in the stable or anywhere, but I do really like my leeks best of all the vegetables that I grow. They are so uncomplaining and adaptable. Like good soldiers, wherever you post them about the vegetable patch, whatever the weather, they thrive, never droop, and salute you with cheerful healthy vigour every morning when you visit them.

Broccoli is quite another case – low morale, un-officerlike, young broccoli plants complain bitterly if you move them, demand constant watering. If the bugs don't get them the pigeons will, despite the latest IT defences – I hang those compact discs that people will send me as bird-scarers. In a bad moment I took a friend's advice and got some ectoplasmic stuff called 'fleece' to keep the cabbage whites off the broccoli – it's ugly, and hell to handle, I'd rather have the bugs.

But leeks haven't an enemy in the world, no animal, no bird, no insect troubles them: all you have to do is occasionally weed round them. I have about two hundred young leeks, all grown from one seed packet, planted out now in sections, platoons and companies – I can't somehow quite think of leeks as cavalry – wherever there is space.

It has been an incredible summer for growth, everything in the vegetable patch is claiming a ridiculously selfish amount of elbowroom. And there has been no sign of the usual truce in the grass war that one counts on being declared for at least part of July and August. This summer it has been mow, mow and boring mow week in week out.

Just for a couple of tropical weeks in July the great ash in our meadow had some reason to look smug: coming very late into leaf in the spring it had seemed to forecast drought. But, since then, we have had equally tropical downpours. Some of the gateways are almost as mucky as they are in winter, and the maize in the fields, to quote one of the laziest and silliest rhymes in all song, is truly "as high as an elephant's eye". Who ever saw an elephant in a cornfield in Oklahoma

"BLACK Children" and "White Children" read two adjacent entries on the village tennis court booking sheet that lives under the veranda in our back yard, earlier this summer. But stand slack you invaluable eagle-eyed Diversity Coordinators and language policepersons, there is no need to dial 999. This isn't an example of the rural racism that the BBC gets so worked up about, it's just that we encourage children to use the tennis court by charging them no more than 50p for a group booking – grown-ups pay a pound a head.

The entries might equally have read Green, Brown, Grey, Sandy or even possibly Gold children, since we have families with those names living hereabouts. Fifty years or so ago there might have been a booking for Pink children, when a Mr Pink was rector of the neighbouring parish. But in fact the court is little more than thirty years old.

It dates from when local government was abolished in the 1970s, we lost our Rural District Council, and the Heath/Walker 'reforms' put the existing munificent gravy train on the rails, giving it such a generous push that I now pay getting on for double every month in Council Tax what I then paid annually in Rates.

When the RDC was dismantled an alert Councillor then living in this village noticed a pot of money going begging, got his hands on it, charmed a gift of land out of its generous owners, and laid down our court. It's a great boon, pays for itself in bookings, and more than forty children are enrolled in the regular Saturday morning coaching sessions conducted by a local saint.

The club, the Glanvilles Wootton Lawn Tennis Club, to give it its grand full name, like so much in this happy village, runs itself really. That is to say a number of us just get on quietly with self-allotted tasks, and meet annually as a committee in Church Farm, with a cat in attendance, as I have earlier described. I do the weed killing, am in charge of bookings, and collect the money. I don't play the game myself; it's too difficult, propelling the ball into that tiny distant postage stamp of a service area just to get a game started. Tennis is for experts... and children.

THE 'Arrivals' area of Terminal 3 at Heathrow Airport is a truly exotic spot, and as strange a place for a country mouse up from Dorset to find himself in as one could readily imagine. That morning I had been riding Dandy in Hay Wood: by the afternoon I was surrounded by every eastern race, from Persian to Chinese, in every from of dress. It was a geography lesson, trying to put labels to them all.

It was also a very interesting study, watching the arrivals being variously greeted as they at last came into view after surviving the frustrations of the baggage hall, immigration and customs and turned the bend into the main concourse.

You should have heard the hoots of scorn and derision I had endured on the previous evening when I had announced at the bridge table that I had decided that, as Othello, my grandson, was now nine years old, he was too old for a kiss, and that I meant to greet him for the first time with a handshake.

In truth I was seeking guidance, and I got it. I was told that at the least I should give the little boy a hug. It was fruitless my saying that he was half Japanese, and that I had noticed that the Japanese were not comfortable being manhandled – a hug it was to be. But I found myself still in a bit of a tizz about it as the long minutes stretched themselves out between their 'plane landing and the moment when I might reasonably expect to pick theirs out amongst the waves of advancing multicoloured faces.

THERE were very wide differences in the modes of greeting. Two English ladies whose encounter took one straight to Luke XV xx "... when he was yet a great way off... saw him... and ran and fell on his neck, and kissed him". It was lovely to see, moving really, I had never before witnessed such unconstrained, unfettered, unfeigned joy in a meeting.

More common, much more common, were the stilted embraces of Levantine men, who lent forward to place one cheek gingerly, reluctantly it seemed, against one cheek of the other, shoulders wrapped for a moment in a stiff, padlock, encircling arm. It was like some avian mating ritual, but not in the least natural. Rarely did it look comfortable or enjoyed.

This drove me to another 'bible', Jane Austen's *Emma*. You may remember when the Knightley brothers greet each other after a separation of some months, at Christmas. "'Howd'ye do George?' and 'John, how are you?' succeeded in the true English style, burying under a calmness that seemed all but indifference the(ir) real attachment...". Jane clearly approved, and so do I. There is a great deal to be said for simply shaking hands, and for leaving what cannot be readily expressed unacted and unsaid.

Well, in due course, there was Miles, and there was dear, shy little Otty, whom I so rarely see, and I gave him a hug: he didn't seem to mind, it was soon all over.

THAT morning I had had a meeting of a very different sort – one of those occasions when the past suddenly pops up and smites you between the eyes – "... it's Lacquer!" the girl had said.

I had seen her, at a distance, riding one, and leading another horse, as Dandy and I turned off Kennels Lane into the track that leads to the field-bound hamlet of Tiley, which has Hay Wood nestling behind it.

We had merely exchanged waves as our ways parted. But then I met her again, coming out of Stonylongs, doing what I thought I was the only person fool enough to do, and making it look easy – managing two big horses, single-handed, through the narrow gateway and passage beside the cattle grid coming off the meadow onto the road; and of course somehow shutting the rather stiff-latched gate behind her.

We chatted, introduced ourselves, and I admired her led horse, an enormous, quality, Irish Draft hunter, just the stamp of my own, much missed, Woody. Then she dropped the bombshell; "You remember this horse...?", she asked, indicating the one she was riding. Of course I immediately did remember... it was Paul's old horse, Paul that died so tragically, and so suddenly. And the details and events of that dreadful time five years ago, unheralded, unasked, rehearsed themselves.

IT IS rather disconcerting when one's wife of many happy years suddenly and unaccountably brings a suitcase down from the attic and starts packing, as Diana had done at the start of the month. But she had her reasons, and there was no cause for alarm. The social silly season in this part of Dorset runs the whole year, but can never have been sillier than it was late this summer. There was everything to be done before we were to get away to visit Louise and her family in Italy.

Autumn seems to have leant forward into August this year, improving what is not my favourite month. We had drenching dews, lovely cool, fly-free early mornings to ride in, yo-yo days of warmth and rain, and, well before we left, many trees were giving notice of the change of season. The chestnuts in the drive, whose scrumptious young spring leaves and budding blossoms the horses used to make a dive for, are looking quite rusty and unappetising, and one of the oaks up on Dungeon is already all over yellow.

Before Othello came, Jasper had paid us a lightening visit. Arriving from a happy day spent at Charmouth. Almost before he was on his feet, out of his mother's car, he was delving in the innumerable pockets of his combat trousers for the fossil he had brought for me, and, almost before that he was asking "Can we make my car?" – we spent much of the first day of his visit in the carpentry shed, before the Supercar was again forgotten.

After the Tennis Club Barbecue, and the Hunt Lunch next day (you get the picture of the social scene?), I suddenly remembered Evensong. Jasper, aged seven now, asked to come with me, and behaved perfectly, standing on the pew seat beside me as usual, sharing my hymnbook, mouthing the puzzling words but coming in with the Amens.

One of the prayers had rather earnestly invoked the congregation's thoughts for the recently dead. Diana told me over supper that he had announced on return from church that he wanted to be burnt when he was dead, and that his ashes were to be spread on the lawn – where he and I had had a lot of fun between times playing rounders and croquet.

OTHELLO and his father arrived on the day the others left (do you begin to understand about the suitcase coming downstairs so early?), and, taking our cue from Jasper's happy account of fossil-hunting, we all went to Charmouth for the day.

I had never been there before, but the place is unbelievably beautiful, uncrowded and unspoilt.... unvisited too by officialdom, there were no notices warning us that the sea is wet, pebbles hard etc, and you are actually allowed to hire a hammer and goggles and go breaking stones hoping to liberate the fossils locked inside them these many million years. There were little groups, children of all ages, dotted here and there on the endless expanse of beach, intent, happy, chipping away.

Such fun, but we barely found a single fossil, and it dawned on us that the plateful sitting on the kitchen table at home, and my new paperweight, all retrieved in triumph from the depths of Jasper's many pockets, had been bought in the beach shop. I must tax him with that when we next speak.

Meanwhile, I really recommend Charmouth bay as a place to take children to. Get there quickly before the Poison Dwarf discovers the perils of the Jurassic Coast and makes everyone wear Chicken-lickin helmets.

WHAT is it about the sound of a distant train that makes it acceptable, welcome even? I once, and once only, strained my ear for the clatter of an approaching helicopter, but surely no one normally craves the sound of air or road traffic – rather, modern life is all struggle to escape it.

It must be some lost memory, some childhood association, like the dash of raindrops against a dark night time window that for ever suggests the wild outdoors, far off adventure, Wuthering Heights, romance. But the sound of a lonely, distant train making its way south, at night, down the leg of Italy, coming across the bay at Santa Marguerita, is music to me.

It is late evening. After the mad scramble of departure, and a marathon of travel, we are once again disengaged for a few days from the adored servitude of home. The lights of Rapallo twinkle across the water, and I dream of Dorset.

AUTUMN REFLECTIONS

ADDED at right-angles to a Tudor longhouse, the front of this rectory was built when George III was on the throne. No doubt at that time it was the very latest thing in domestic architecture, the height of fashion and convenience, announcing to the world and especially to his visitors that Parson Thomas Fox knew what was what, and that he could afford it.

However, a successor in the parish, as I have always supposed bullied by his wife or daughters at the height of the lawn tennis craze, turfed over the carriage sweep, turning the house back-to-front. No one comes to our front door now unless they are lost. It was a chance arrangement that has worked out very happily, giving us a secluded peaceful lawn.

Originally thatched, but otherwise I guess, apart from the vegetation, looking now much as on the day it was built, the house, like a human face, takes is character on first acquaintance from its windows. Sash windows, no doubt a very clever invention in their day, are beautiful but a bore. They let the rain in almost as efficiently as they admit light.

Whenever this dear old house stands blinded by one of the south-westerly gales that every now and then roar up to us across the downland from the sea, seeming to pick on us as I used sometimes to fancy, the windows rattle and weep inconsolably. Then we have to rush round with towels, to keep the water off the floors and out of ceilings. I suppose that it is something you have to live with if you are so lucky as to live in a Georgian house, like the single small fault that one must just put up with in womanly perfection.

TENNIS on our lawn, even the tamest of vicarage lawn tennis, has long been out of the question, not least for fear of putting out those pretty eyes. Also, until a few years ago an enormous copper beech, no doubt planted by that same Parson Fox as part of the old house's eighteenth century makeover, used to dominate the lawn: you could see it from miles around.

Originally pollarded, its giant muscular arms spread out from its massive stunted trunk. At night, even in the lightest air, it whispered to the house – comfortingly, or alarmingly, depending on the cast of the child-hood mind. In a rising breeze it soughed and sighed, and in a gale it moaned and howled stupendously. And of course it had a swing suspended from it, and its capacious fork was a place for children to get to and hide in, if they could but escape the grownups.

Unlike oaks, beeches don't live for ever, and one of the saddest things I have had to do here was have that great beech tree down when, like so many of its contemporaries up on the cap of Dungeon Hill, it died of old age. Fortunately, in my parents' time a seedling had been found growing in the vegetable garden – I believe that this is impossible with a hybrid, but it happens to be true – and, taking no chances, they had it professionally planted, by Scott's of Merriot, vis-à-vis its parent on the opposite corner of the lawn.

This is now handsome, half-grown, well on the way to being a replacement for its parent, to feed the fantasies of future generations of over-imaginative children, well up to concealing the odd bird's-nest and supporting a child's swing, and once again a homing landmark from all the high ground around.

JUST as they proclaim its age, the windows explain the geography of the house. Two almost cube rooms on the ground floor are a drawing and a dining room, the two main bedrooms over them with a dressing room squeezed between, and above again two children's attic bedrooms, which double as my work rooms.

On nobody's route to anywhere, the attic rooms are just made for writing: not for me the inconvenience that Jane Austen suffered from of collecting and protecting her thoughts in the heart of a busy family house, and having patiently to close her desk as soon as she heard an approaching step, or the click of a door latch.

The dining room, on the left as you look at the house, was in my father's day his study, lined with books from floor to ceiling, and with tables stacked with great folios and tomes that wouldn't fit on any shelf. He had a wonderful library, and I loved his books, I could enter that room in the dark and put my finger on the spine of many a favourite.

When he died, in 1968, at the ludicrous age of sixty-one, I was away with my regiment in Germany. Someone, who evidently scanned the death announcements in the newspapers, came tap-tapping at the door and asked my mother if by any chance she had any books she didn't want. Believing that she was short of money, which she wasn't, and thinking that she would have to leave the house, which she didn't, she let him take the best of that precious library, for a nominal sum. If I shut my eyes I can picture many of them today, and miss them still.

My father had a wonderfully skilled hand and eye. He could make or draw anything, nothing in that line too difficult for him. When we first came to the house, in 1951, it was in a dreadful state of disrepair. He had each one of those nine sash windows out of their cases and onto his bench, remade them, re-hung them, cords weights and all, so that they opened and shut sweetly, and as near as possible kept out the rain. People tell me that I am uncannily like my father; the resemblance is entirely superficial, I couldn't begin to do joinery like that.

SET in the path, immediately in front of the doorstep, when we first arrived here, was to be found a large slab of sandstone about two feet square, having a small rectangular hole, like a tummy button, in its centre in which a metal tag was located. How this mysterious stone, with its strange naval 'key', had defied the curiosity of past generations of rectors, let alone their children is itself a mystery.

Surely they must have wondered, as we did, what lay beneath it? Was it only another well, or was it perhaps an entrance to an underground passage leading to the church, was there not some dark secret to be uncovered? I know they wondered, one of them returning to her childhood home has told me so, but how could they bear not to lift the stone?

We, you may be sure, wasted no time about it. What several generations of rectors, their families and their visitors had trodden as the first step into or out of the house turned out to be the back of a memorial tablet from the church, thrown out during the Victorian 'restoration', when the entire north wall, found to be footed on nothing more secure than a line of rotting coffins, had to be demolished and rebuilt. Evidently the stone had caught some provident eye, been salvaged, and placed face-down as paving.

The enigmatic 'key' was there to hold securely in place an octagonal slate centrepiece, now broken, and from which all the writing had been long since erased. The stone surround, heavily carved, typically seventeenth century, with crossed bones and other Hogarthian mementi mori, is now a birdbath in the old rose garden.

So, whatever life the stone originally commemorated, it again, after years of trampling, has some memorial as well as a useful function. The garden birds are very grateful, and they make a pretty show when they come to wash and drink under the window of the old Tudor kitchen, which is now our main livingroom.

We were to discover other treasures ejected from the church when the young architect Thomas Hardy supervised its 'restoration' – I keep the quotes because, as Hardy himself came to recognise and regret, in many cases, desecration might have been a more appropriate term for what, with the best intentions, Victorians did to medieval churches.

In odd corners of the garden we found bits of discarded carved Ham stone tracery from old church windows, which it has been a great pleasure to find new uses for, to build-in to masonry here and there about the place, and to think how those storied stones may been caressed by the countless thousand wrapt or inattentive glances of worshipers in past centuries.

Best of all was a stone, slightly smiling face that surfaced, ghost-like, one day in the vegetable garden. It is a recognisable and characterful portrait of who knows whom, no doubt a fragment of a monument to some long dead squire. It now hangs in a place of honour in the house.

"Help!"

ENTER the house by the front door and walk straight ahead, after a few paces passing through another door that now stands permanently open into the old servants' quarters, and you find yourself in the back hall with its array of bells. Goodness only knows when one of them was last rung, as no doubt it was occasionally, in anger: but they still hang there, poised on their curled springs, ostensibly attentive, obedient, ready for a summons by a long dead hand.

This place was not designed to be run single-handed. The last Incumbent lived like Robinson Crusoe, marooned by social progress or decline, depending how you view the history of the last century. The house was in makeshift disrepair, in part almost a ruin – you could have hoist a bus through the hole in the stone stable roof – surrounded by jungle, the lawn a hayfield. "It was like Sleeping Beauty's garden" my mother always said.

From the day we came here, right up until last year, the village has supplied an unbroken dynasty of help, sometimes singly, sometimes a couple working indoors and out. It would be invidious to name names, nearly all are still alive, all became friends, most still are neighbours.

Age and fashion have taken their toll, and that old well is dry: now we are visited weekly by a flying squad. Kate and Charlotte comprise the A Team, I call them the 'the Jollies'. They descend on us like a small flock of chattering birds, happy birds. I like to hear them about the house, making the best of their work, even if they chase me mercilessly from room to room.

I am old enough to remember cap, apron, functioning bell-pull, the odd curtsey even – although perhaps I am imagining that from my mother's stories of her childhood: it is the defining feature of my generation, we remember 'before the war', but I cannot regret those times, and am wholeheartedly glad that they are gone.

ONE of the nice things about living in what was once the rectory is that you know the names of all those who lived there before, a roll of Rectors is posted in the church. I don't suppose that John Sprot, installed in 1302, lived in this actual house, and his successor Galfrid de Wermondesworth, 1326, sounds like a pluralist absentee, but I feel fairly confident that by the time Thomas Mew was rector (1639-73), he and his family would have been living in what are now the back-quarters of the house, my favourite part of it.

Inside a window shutter of one of the Georgian bedrooms are marked the heights of various children. The oldest entry, the one nearest to the ground, reads "Cyril, Sep 5th, 1873, three years old", and we can trace his growth, and that of his siblings, Eva, Sybil, Bobby and Norman, until he was five foot ten on his seventeenth birthday, in 1887. The roll in the church tells us that they were children of the Woodman family who held the rectory, father and son, from 1857 until 1891.

Another feature, and again a pleasant one, is that the descendants of past rectors sometimes visit us, some having known the place in their childhood, their memories helping us to piece together fragments of the history of the village, neighbours, house and garden.

One man, who called on us a couple of years ago, told of how his parents met and fell in love, his father spotting his future wife out of that very window where the Woodman children's heights are listed, whilst she took part in a village pageant on the lawn in his grandfather's time as rector. His name was Tod: this parish seems to have had rather a lot of monosyllabic rectors, in name at least – I doubt their sermons were so short.

BUT you cannot live in an old rectory, or certainly not live in this one, and deny the church. Just a few paces beyond the orchard wall its tower stands over us; its vane forecasts the weather every morning; its tall face reflects the setting sun, sometimes indescribably beautifully, any cloudless evening; its bells tell us it is Thursday night, when the ringers practise, and of course remind us where we should be and when on Sunday.

At the annual Fête, and when there are big weddings or well attended funerals, there is always a polite request for the meadow or paddock to be used as a car park, and people walk to and from church up our drive. If you find that sort of thing tiresome, then a rectory is not for you.

I was for a short inglorious time Church Warden. The Rector was a dear friend, and enormous help with my writing, as there wasn't much that he didn't know about venery, in fact he was also an MFH, but I never hit it off with the hierarchy, and I came to blows with the then Archdeacon.

I had had the temerity to install a badly needed new heating system in the church without first seeking permission or getting the correct piece of paper – I know it's very wicked and I shall probably burn in hell for it, but I don't have much patience with that sort of thing – and was hauled before the Chancellor of the Diocese in a Consistory Court. We won our case, but it was a disillusioning experience, and expensive, it cost the parish £400 in legal fees. Fresh out of the Army I had ingrained ideas about what authority owes to its subordinates in the way of friendly encouragement, loyalty, and support: the church it seemed to me turned these values on their head.

I wasn't sacked, but I was glad to quit office, and am now just a rather bolshie lay vice chairman of the PCC, sidesman, lesson reader when asked, and I attempt to sing the bass line in the choir when there is one, sometimes being the only man to do so.

At parish level, my sole unhappiness is that new, to my mind very inferior, liturgy and versions of the Bible, are driving out old, much more beautiful texts. I am afraid that this will eventually drive me out too: but I shall still love our church, and think it a great stroke of luck to live almost in its shadow and under its benign gaze.

SHERBORNE, with its 1300-year-old abbey, schools, and single gently descending street is happily no clone town, to use a term much in the news as I write; that is to say it has not lost its old, distinctive character, or its longstanding family businesses. You can hardly walk ten paces up or down Cheap Street without a neighbour greeting you, and behind most counters are familiar friendly faces: Sherborne has more the nature of a village than a town. It is where we shop, unless some dire exigency drives us to visit Dorchester or Yeovil.

When we lived briefly at Buckland Newton we were drawn south to shop in the county town, but an invisible watershed divides that large village from this small one, although they are only twenty minutes ride apart: Glanvilles Wootton looks north to Sherborne, and we are thankful for it. I sometimes see escapees from the gravitational pull of Dorchester, no doubt guiltily, shopping in Sherborne, when they have no right at all to be there – it does not surprise me. Sherborne is perfect, it is country, it is small-scale, and a bit behind the times.

At the top of Cheap Street is to found Olivers Coffee House where, at a long timber-topped table, you may sit on a high stool, watch the world go by through the old shop window, read the newspaper, or, if you are a journalist with a taste for dialogue, pretend to read whilst listening to how people talk.

Sometimes when I am in Olivers there is a gathering of what I call the Boys' Brigade, a clutch of old young men, pensioners I guess, who look out for each other, get together, and have a jolly, chatty time. "Morning men!" one of them might typically say in greeting his playmates as he comes in off the street. It is a joy to see and hear them at it.

As you descend Cheap Street its several charity shops, which have long since displaced my London tailor, cry out to be visited, just in case there is some irresistible bargain to be had. When I have time on my hands I often 'draw' the street, as if it were a long fox-covert, a certain 'find'. Or I might never get to Sherborne, without first checking out the dump at the foot of Dancing Hill.

The dump is like a Battersea Dogs Home for discarded chattels; they sit on trestle tables, appealing for new owners, begging to be taken home. There you may pick up for a few pennies all sorts of thing you need, but perhaps didn't know you needed until you saw them. It is a branch of recycling that is not only virtuous but is also fun.

I bought my de Jongh view of Old London Bridge at the dump, thinking it was a Canaletto; recently promoted from the summerhouse, it now hangs in my dressing room. And at the dump, just the other day, I bought for 30p an enormous old calf-bound Prayer Book and Bible; it was starting to rain, and I just could not bear to turn my back and leave it lying there.

Printed in Oxford, the date on the title page is 1732, it is much of an age with the front of this house. There is still a marker between the pages left by the last person to use it. Its front and back boards just hang on, but one day, when I am in funds, I mean to take it to the binders.

SELF-respect is a fine and necessary thing, 'self esteem', as we see all round us, a disaster. How on earth did it come about that we allowed self-worship to become the touchstone of well-being, when, in fact, and obviously, it is the plumb opposite of anything that might pass for a recipe for happiness, and is the death of grace, loving kindness, consideration and good manners?

These rather grim reflections recur again and again to me whenever I go out into any public place – whether it is the litter in our lanes, or the insouciance of people one encounters in the street... even, rarely, in Sherborne.

If these are over-gloomy thoughts, it is good to remember examples of quite opposite behaviour that, especially in the young, are like sudden bursts of sunshine. I think of Louise, the young lady in Rules, the Cheap Street stationers, who told me which way the accent went on *pardonnèz* when I went in to enquire, and who laughed when I asked if there was any charge for accents – so few young laugh easily. Is there I wonder a connection between the loss of a sense humour and the loss of manners?

There was the skinhead on the London train who, with the pleasantest smile, when he had done with it, handed me his copy of *The Star* to read – I did my best to seem appreciative, and to appear to study it with interest. And the Hazelbury Bryan fodder merchant, a total stranger to me, who, when we had loaded my purchases in the back of the Landrover and I found my pockets empty said "Don't worry, we remember your father here, just send a cheque" – my father, their doctor evidently, died more than three decades ago. It was a job not to weep.

Surely it is possible to value style without discounting substance? In public life at least, we seem to have lost both. But perhaps what I miss most of all is what, for want of a better word, I call grace – that ineffable but indispensable quality. Why do people take themselves, and every little thing, perhaps inadvertently said or done, so seriously: why so deadly humourless, why so ready to be hurt, why so po-faced, so glum: is it really such a tax to laugh and smile?

"IT WOULD kill you to leave this house", a neighbour and old friend said to me once. It is not true of course, but it was a useful exaggeration, helping one to face up to what must happen sometime, and, hopefully, to do so with the minimum of fuss and self-pity. He had come to talk to me about his ordination studies, but evidently we had drifted onto other topics, and I must have given voice to a thought that is seldom far from my mind these days.

I was working in the summerhouse in the old rose-garden when he called, which means almost certainly that it was not summertime. Far better called a sun house, it is unbearable in hot weather, but bliss on a sunny day at almost any other time of year: I often work there. My parents loved a summerhouse, and this is the third they had that I remember.

My earliest memory almost is of the summerhouse in our garden at South Petherton, in Somerset, where we lived before the war. It was where I first learnt to read, under a governess, and it stood beside a grass tennis court. Once, when my mother, who, thanks to schooling at Roedean was very sportive, had a tennis party, I, aged five or six, must have been winging and making a nuisance of my self. My father, the gentlest of men, then in his twenties, bopped me on the head with a rolled-up *BMJ*, and said "Dry up!". No doubt I did.

Lucky there were no lurking social workers to spirit me off into 'care'. But the question that does lurk is, why did my father take a copy of the

British Medical Journal to a tennis party? The answer of course is that he hoped to be surplus to requirements with the racquet, and to have a chance to study.

Like his three sons, he was hopelessly inept at games; but he was deeply serious about his work, absolutely devoted to it. His third name was Ernest, and earnest he was, as his patients, who adored him, had reason to be thankful for, and as, even now I am still frequently reminded.

∽◊◡

AFTER the war, when he was released by the Army, my father bought a practice in this county – the nearest to his old one that professional etiquette allowed – and we lived for a time in the old doctor's house in the next village to this. There he built a summerhouse, and had it thatched, so that I might lie out-of-doors, when, at the age of twelve, I was struck down with rheumatic fever.

In those days, I don't know if it is still the case, rheumatic fever meant three months lying prone, not even sitting up: the slightest exertion was believed to threaten damage to the heart. My parents collected me, lying in the back seat of a taxi, from the Oxford hospital where I had been rushed, in my final term, from my horrified prep school.

Morning, noon and night, between his visits and his surgeries, my desperately busy father carried me from night room, to day room and, when the weather allowed, to the summerhouse. What is more, he gave up his evenings to reading his favourite authors to me, hour on hour. In a sense you might say that I was born in a summerhouse.

∽◊◡

OUR summerhouse here knocks spots off both the others. It is in the north-east corner of a small garden-within-a-garden, enclosed by house, wall and two hedges, its special glory an ancient medlar tree. If the old front of the house is private, this, once a labour-intensive rose-garden, is positively secret, hidden as it is behind the original Tudor longhouse.

Where was once a formal arrangement of beds is now a small lawn, with a deep flower border against a ten foot wall on one side, facing a thicket of shrubs, ground elder and illicit bluebells on the other. Set on rollers on a circular rail, the summerhouse can be turned this way and that, to catch or to avoid the sun. It's a real treasure.

Sitting there on a rare sunny morning late this last May it was a joy to watch the comings and goings of the garden's birds. Blackbirds were busy feeding their brood in the cotoneaster on the house wall, and just a few paces away a spotted flycatcher was starting to build in the wisteria – hurrah, I had thought that the flycatchers had deserted us – and, damn them, jackdaws were busy diving down and popping out of the kitchen chimney. I just don't understand what supports their nest in a smooth-sided flue, or how they survive the fumes from an oil-fired boiler that 'comes up' twice a day to heat the water.

Hanging behind me, as I write there now, is a large, battered, unframed canvas, an oil painting done well over a hundred years ago, and rescued by my father from an old powdered-milk factory that used to serve as a village hall in Buckland Newton. He had an eye for such things. If the picture, once a fine piece of work, ever had a title it must have been "The Lecture".

A frock-coated man is addressing a group, the ladies in Edwardian or Victorian dresses seated, the men standing – the atmosphere, the ennui, the scents and the sounds are palpable. It is a very cleverly executed picture, with quite a strong suggestion of satire in it, but is sadly completely beyond rescue or repair. I would just love to know its origin, how it fell into such neglect. It pleases me no end that we are able to give it some sort of home, where it lives on, enjoyed, the unknown artist's skill appreciated, but we couldn't possibly hang it anywhere but in the summerhouse.

That time when my neighbour Michael came to see me here to talk about his ordination plans, it caused me to turn over in my mind yet again how we must one day leave this lovely rambling place; it has far too much roof, too many rooms, and too much ground for just the pair of us. But I ended my ruminations as I generally do by thinking that as long as we have our health and our horses we will probably stay put. We give ourselves ten more years… the trouble is we say that every passing year.

NO PART of this place is more strongly redolent of my mother than the small rose-garden, which was so easily hived off and made specifically hers when my father died and we divided up the house. She lived throughout her long widowhood in the Tudor wing that overlooks it, by courtesy, through all those years, known as The Dower House.

Although the youngest but one of the nine children of a Norfolk rectory, and having five equally strong-minded and characterful sisters, she was not cut out to play second fiddle. Whatever she did, she was usually in the lead, or conveniently close behind whoever was.

Whilst she lived, and she survived all her siblings, like a coach-driver holding a fistful of reins, she kept in touch with every known member of an almost innumerable family spread worldwide. This is a function that lapsed with her death four years ago, and is much missed.

She was a power in the village too, in her day. She sits in the centre of the front row of our millennium group picture, who else? As the plaque on it records, she opened our small children's playground charmingly named Dear Leap. Known to one and all as Granny Grace, she was a remarkable woman.

One of my earliest memories is of her playing the part of Duke Orsino, or it might even have been Romeo, in a production by some South Petherton women's drama group. My mother adored acting, never stopped acting some would say. But it would not be said unkindly. Although she was what we might today call feisty, she was not a person who inspired unkindness. Quite the opposite, people loved her.

IF MY father set my cast of mind, taught me to use my hands and to care a great deal about horses, my mother set the course of my life. "You won't think of going into the Army, will you?", she said to me one day during the school holidays, knowing full well that I was in a state of mind to be steered. She always had a hand to play, and always played it cannily. So much for my 'career guidance' as a schoolboy – it wanted only for my House Tutor back at Clifton to tell me which regiment I was to join.

My first term at Sandhurst was somewhat complicated by my father's conviction that I needed to have a horse with me there. Anyone who has endured the chaotic first weeks of the Junior Term at the Royal Military Academy, or indeed read of Prince Harry's recent experience of it, will appreciate what an unworldly decision my father's was. He visited me during my first week-end there, did a recce of the stables, and ordained that I was to have Duchess, his second string hunter, and that I was to come home and collect her as soon as Sandhurst's strict regime for juniors allowed.

Fetching Duchess from Dorset was to prove something of an adventure. It involved riding her at first light to Sherborne station, a long day spent in a magnificently solid rail horsebox, for ever being decoupled from various trains, shunted into sidings here and there, more than once fancying ourselves forgotten, and eventually being deposited at Blackwater station in pitch darkness, with, yet ahead of us, a terrifying walk up the even then busy A30, blinding headlights everywhere.

I can never forget Corporal Donohoe of the 4th/7th Dragoon Guards who was my groom at the Staff College stables. Very Irish, very horsy, very knowing, very fly, he was just the sort of introduction that a school-boy needed to the ethos of a cavalry regiment. Between us we somehow managed to keep Duchess exercised; poor thing, there were no loose-boxes, she stood in a stall as I remember. I only pray that I had the wit to tip him, and to tip him generously: I doubt I did, I was as green as green could be.

If my father's insistence on mounting me at Sandhurst was unworldly, but for the fact that he was by nature utterly straightforward, it could have been Machiavellian. Instead of playing rugger on Wednesday afternoons, it did me no harm at all to be hunting with the Drag, rubbing shoulders with the Commandant, Major General David Dawnay, occasionally hacking home with him. I have little doubt that, at least in part, I have my father and Duchess to thank for my eventually passing out 6th in my term.

"WHAT about the men's tea meal?" our Company Commander at Sandhurst used to ask whenever we cadets were trotting out an answer to any military problem set us. We laughed at him on the quiet, but not at his medals; and, as you can see, his rather quaint locution has stayed with me as an admirable expression of the keystone of an army officer's life, that the welfare of the men under his command always comes first. In an old cavalry regiment of course, the horses were to be thought of even before the men.

The word 'regimentation', with its pejorative, Prussian associations, is a libel on the British army. I never knew such freedom as I enjoyed with my regiment, where you were given a job to do, were trusted to do it, were judged by results, and nobody stood over you. It was, I have no doubt still is, the antithesis of today's 'liberal' society, where nothing is left to com-monsense or honour, no-one is trusted, and every atom of joy and satis-faction is squeezed out of work; particularly, and particularly sadly, in non-military professions such as medicine and teaching.

Chance, and my mother's benign stratagem, had taken me into a life that I was in many ways quite unsuited for. The Army's physical and its social demands were both beyond me, I was useless at games, could never run as fast as my sister, couldn't throw a cricket ball, and found much of mess life, except for playing cards, excruciating. But the decision, if you can call it that, turned out to be a great stroke of luck.

The Army as a whole, but more especially a regiment, and more espe-cially still a line cavalry regiment, is, contrary to its public image, extraor-dinarily tolerant of, and kind to, misfits: it fits them in. It is the special genius of good regiments to discover such qualities as you may have, put them to use, and to cover for you where you lack.

My regiment, then the 13th/18th Royal Hussars (Queen Mary's Own), in effect said to me when I arrived in 1954 "You're odd but you'll do", and took me to its bosom. There I nestled very happily for some twenty years until, after commanding, I was turned out upon the world again, in due course to find something else congenial to do. It was all luck.

IT WAS lucky also that my soldiering was all strictly of the peacetime sort; I never saw a battle, let alone a war. Although I was several times in what was technically an operational theatre, as far as I know I was only once shot at, and only once really felt myself to be in danger.

The single bullet that went splat just beside me against the armour of a Ferret scout-car, was fired, at a great range I think, from the Jebel Akhdhar, the Green Mountain, the rebel stronghold in the Oman where the Sultan's enemies held out. A very young, and very temporary captain, I was commanding two troops of my regiment, on detachment, 1200 miles away from my Squadron HQ in Aden, itself detached from the Regiment in Germany.

My two troops were at that time I believe the only all-British military presence in the Sultanate. Our job was to try to keep open an important route, you could barely call it a road, that ran through rock desert inland from the capital, Muscat: the rebels continually mined it, and made life uncomfortable for those not of their political persuasion.

A tiny HQ and one troop were camped in front of a Beau Geste mud fort outside Muscat, at a place called Bait al Falaj, my other troop at the far end of the 'road', at a place called Nizwa, where Sayid Tariq, a half-brother of the Sultan ruled. He was, so I am told by someone who knew him a lot better than I did, an English and German-speaking graduate, Beethoven fan, and bridge-player. To my young eyes he was just someone who looked like Henry VIII dressed up as Lawrence. I did get to ride one of his horses – I am glad that I have ridden an Arab in Arabia – she was tiny, scrawny, but full of character and go.

Occasionally a small 'plane was provided to fly me from one end of my small 'empire' to the other. It was real *Boys Own Paper* soldiering, I'm ashamed that I did not enjoy it more, but the desert had no message for me. Apart from my soldiers, I was entirely on my own, was lonely, loathed the climate, and thought a great deal of Dorset, the horse I had left behind me, and the hunting I was missing.

Here, if you will kindly allow for the jejune utterances of a boy just four days past his twenty-fifth birthday, is an excerpt from a letter home, dated 17 March, 1958....

"Thank you very much ... for 'The Uneven Road' and 'Woodstock'..
they came as a delightful surprise, and met me in the middle of
nowhere.... Since I last wrote to you I have travelled many, many
miles, not without adventure.... On Thursday we went in convoy
from Bait al Falaj to Nizwa. As the crow goes this is only 90,
but the road journey is 130 miles. It was a most spectacular drive,
most of the way under the shadow of the Green Mountain. This is
where Talib, the rebel leader, lives with his army of bandits. We had
a brush with him on the way up... and on the way back lost a
vehicle on one of his mines. No-one was hurt, nor is anyone likely
to be in this comic opera war.
The two books found me...just after the mine incident. I opened the
parcel about an hour later sitting under the shade of a large rock
waiting for our kettle to boil for lunch..."

THE one time that I got really scared was right at the end of my regimental service, in Ireland. Very foolishly, I, who had no business doing such a thing, went walkabout with just my single escort, in an unsavoury part of the city of Armagh, hoping to find a cache of arms, explosives or whatnot. Soon a crowd of children gathered, they started to pick up stones, began to pelt us. We both of us of course had loaded weapons, which in many ways was the most horrifying aspect of the situation: there was nothing for it but to run.

My time in Ireland was without exception the most interesting, demanding and rewarding soldiering that I did. Lucky for me, again that word lucky, that it came in my last four months service with my regiment: it was as if the previous twenty years had been designed as preparation for it – which I suppose is exactly what they were.

We had left our tanks in Germany, were in a mainly infantry role, and were there to keep the peace. Unlike training for the next World War, it seemed extra-ordinarily worthwhile.

THE GREAT fireplace in what Arthur Mee, in his King's England series, called the 'Tudor kitchen' in the back quarters of this house was bricked-in and invisible when we first came here. But my father had a workman put a pickaxe through the hollow wall, and there it was, almost a little room of its own, hidden for no one knew how long.

Why it had been bricked in was no mystery. No doubt the fashion of the day – sash windows, Adam over-mantles and so on – frowned on such barbaric relics as great smoky, dangerous open fires. What was a puzzle was why the oak beam was missing. Perhaps some inattentive scullion had allowed a spark to settle there, the beam had caught, and smouldered beyond rescue: or, more likely, the 'improving' builder removed it, a valuable piece of salvage, and it is doing duty in some cottage hereabouts.

You can get a flavour of this sort of thing in *Persuasion*, when Jane Austen's heroine, Anne Elliot, regrets some of the old comfortable domestic arrangements swept out by Georgian modernity. And you have to smile when you reflect how each generation knows best, stands on its head what stood on its feet before, only for the next brood of ever-so-knowing children in their turn to up-end it once more – repaints expensively stripped woodwork and so on. How long before somebody bricks in "that ugly old fireplace" again?

Indeed, I plead guilty myself, and you can laugh at me, for installing the brick inner fireplace that you may see there now. The cavernous grate was too much for my mother to manage in her old age, when, in her widowhood, this became her living room. An arrangement in a Dordogne farmhouse caught my eye, I sketched it, gave it to the gifted local bricky to construct – so what you see today is a little bit of vernacular agricultural France. It works well, we like it, but no doubt someone, some day, will take a pickaxe to it.

IT IS in this one-time kitchen that, appropriately enough, we play bridge. We are not fanatics, but play once or twice a month, with great enjoyment, for tuppenny points, nothing serious. My parents had no idea of playing cards, had no card-sense whatever. But more metropolitan cousins, staying for Christmas perhaps, would bring with them ideas and fashions from the great world outside Dorset, canasta and so on, the latest thing.

I came to love card games. Is there anything to beat the thrill of the moment when you pick up your newly dealt hand with, until you actually see it, its infinite possibilities, promise and allure? Poker got hold of me briefly when I first joined my regiment, but I got a fright and foreswore the game. I learnt to play bridge when four of us used to sneak off the tank-park, and hide in a back room in the mess. Our instructor, later to command a squadron for me, is now a general.

Through from this room is a real kitchen, latterly my mother's, now only rarely in use, when we are entertaining at full stretch and there is serious cooking going on. I call it Mrs Brigg's kitchen, as we have a fancy to equip it in the Edwardian style.

An old schoolroom clock that I bought at auction permanently says that it is just past lunch-time – I must get it mended – and there are old implements, some, like the toffee-hammer, given by kind friends. Open on a cast-iron stand with little weights to keep the pages open, which I found at the dump, is my great-grandmother's cookery book.

Through again to a back hall, hanging on the tall wall over the stairs, is the funeral hatchment with my mother's arms on it that I had made as a memorial to her. Like Michael Henchard, but for different reasons, she wouldn't have a grave.

They are lovely arms, a diamond lozenge with three greyhounds running flat out on a scarlet field. In the top quarter, on black, are two York roses and a knobbly cross, *Pommé* or *Botonné*, I'm not sure which - my apologies to York Herald who drew the thing.

My mother's family were proud of their warrior descent, she and each one of her eight siblings was christened Eliott-Drake. Drake we all know about; General Eliott it was who saved Gibraltar from the Spaniards, so that the Rock might become a pebble in the shoe of New Labour, as I like to think. You can see a replica of the Keys of Gibraltar hanging in the ingle nook, on the right, in Becky Unwin's picture.

I can neither forget, nor take too seriously these claims of blood. When my mother became engaged to the best of men, a grand, titled cousin whispered about that she was marrying 'an apothecary'. His family, we presume originating in Scandinavia, once made pins and files very successfully in Warrington, but sadly the business was long since sold up.

I'm a great believer in hybrid vigour: remember Perdita?

I JUST love this old room, which was the dining room in my parents' day – my father, as I told you, had the Georgian dining room for his books. I have spent so many hours sitting here, as one did, over family meals, usually three generations present, often a selection of our myriad cousins staying. It must have been in this room that my weekly letters home, from wherever I was with my regiment, were opened and first read. I found them all, every one of them, in a tin box in the attic.

It is when I am sitting in this room, in a work chair that I have tucked away in one corner, that I most dread leaving the place. The sun floods in on a cloudless morning, and in the evening gently illuminates the church tower, which is framed by its east-facing broad mullioned window.

The room was cleared after my mother died. By a long-standing and happy arrangement all her things went to my younger brother, so Diana and I have filled it and fitted it out anew, to our own taste. It is a dream room, every-where in it that I look is some loved thing, some memory, or some thing especially got for its particular place, like my father's portrait of a favourite horse over the fireplace.

By me, where I sit, usually with a book to review whilst I and the horses digest breakfast, I have two special pictures – sketches by John Gould. One is in pencil, of a wren, the other a group of parakeets, in which he has tried out various poses, different colours, and left his hastily scrawled instructions to the artist who was to make a finished picture of it: he was always in a hurry.

As well as being my father's great-grandfather, John Gould was a great man in his day. A Dorset gardener's son, born in poverty almost, he rose to be a Fellow of the Royal Society, a world figure in his field: his books fetch enormous sums, his images of birds are everywhere, and everywhere treasured. I am immensely proud of him.

AS WELL as those two favourite pictures, I have in that same corner ready to hand all the books that I most often need to look into, from *Baily's Hunting Directory* to the Bible. And I have a CD player – such a wonderful invention – 'compact' discs indeed, so much of my favourite music stored in so small a compass.

Like Tweedledum and Tweedledee, words and music have fought a duel for my affections through all my life. If music had rather a thin time of it during my army service, and words seem to have won in the end, music was my first love.

Ours was a musical household. My mother had a trained voice, and some of my earliest childhood recollections are of sitting on the piano stool beside her whilst she played and sang ballads that were popular in the 1930s, "Charlie is my Darling", "Who Will Buy my Coloured Herring" and "Speed Bonny Boat". And at Clifton I came under the influence of a great teacher, the one-armed Dr Douglas Fox, whose memory is still strongly with me; such a courageous, inspiring man was he.

As for words, I have already told of how my father fed my young mind with his favourite authors, Fielding, Smollett, Dickens, Scott and Surtees. When I left home, wherever I was, he mailed me paperbacks, almost weekly – the package that caught up with me in the Omani desert was typical, an old favourite, Scott's *Woodstock*, and something a bit more mind-widening, Belhaven's *Uneven Road*.

In due course my own taste in books developed. Unaided either by school or my father, I discovered Jane Austen, whom I think of as the most admirable stylist in our language, as well as being a great moralist. That tragically short-lived spinster still teaches us how we ought to live… with restraint, a cool eye – cooler than I have command of – and, yes, sense and sensibility rather than pride and prejudice. In so far as I can read into it in her books, I worship that woman's mind.

Best of all of course is when words and music memorably combine. I write this under the recent influence of an electrifying performance of Verdi's *Macbeth* in Holland Park. Forget the worthy efforts of the Italian librettist, forget the flashing surtitles, think just of the words put by Shakespeare into MacDuff's mouth in his heartbroken lament, "What all my pretty chickens and their dam at one fell swoop?", and hear what Verdi makes of them in one of the greatest tenor arias in all opera.

Or, more contemplatively, Houseman's words – he was for many years a favourite – set to Sibelius's music… *Be still my soul*. Could anyone plagued with a questing, turbulent mind ask for better remedy: for conveying profound feeling, is there anything to beat well-chosen Anglo-Saxon monosyllables?

IF PAST rectors kept saddle horses, or rode to hounds, there was little sign of it when we came here, one, Mr Smith (1905-1925), just in living memory, rode a tricycle round his parish. But there was only standing for horses in the stable, useless old-fashioned stalls, and the village bier lived in the coach-house: there were no loose boxes, no mounting block, and, worst of all, there was a great hole in the stable roof.

One of the first things we did when we arrived was to set about putting this all to rights. It was always so with my father, wherever we lived, getting horses and stabling for them was almost his first concern. During the 'phoney war', in 1939/40, after he had sold up in Somerset to volunteer for the RAMC and we had no permanent home, my mother rented an old mill house at Stock in Essex, near where my father was in camp.

He had fitted out a stable, got a horse over from his brother in Hampshire, was planning to hunt, when he was sent off as MO on a troop-ship, and spent the rest of the war afloat, successfully dodging U-boats. My mother was less fortunate, the mill house managed to attract a stray bomb in the Battle of Britain: it was demolished, she, my sister and grandmother were extremely lucky to survive. I and my elder brother were away at school, my younger brother not yet born.

When my father was demobilized and bought this practice, and we lived for a while in the rather cramped, landless doctor's house in the next village, he borrowed stabling, went off to Taunton market to buy himself a hunter. Rather like beanstalk Jack in the fairy story, he came back with two. Ever the optimist, he had bought a showy chestnut mare for my mother, who was as likely to hunt as she was to fly.

The mare evidently took his fancy, as she did most people until they rode her: like many horses looking for an owner immediately post-war, she was useless, and his own grey mare that came with her was little better. It was to be several years before he got suited with a decent hunter: the best quad we had in our stable was a skewbald pony that he bought for £40 for my sister and me.

That proved to be a brilliant buy. Punch, who came from the neighbouring parish of Folke, never turned his head, and taught us to enjoy hunting. Ten years later my sister married Punch's previous owner. They were married for nearly fifty years.

THE mounting block that my father and I built has been, in a sense, rather more than that to me - something of a school-bench. Like, I guess, so many that are born flat-footed, inept and weedy, useless at ballgames, I have found myself lent wings when in the saddle. Horses, for better or worse, have to a great extent, made me what I am. If you find the subject boring, bear with me just a fraction more whilst I try to explain.

It's not just the fun you get from riding them, it's what you learn from them about life's give and take. If you have read this far you will already know that I loathe 'back seat driving' – the boss who doesn't trust you, the official who seeks to prescribe every little thing you do, and the way you are to do it.

Horses have taught me the value of the loose rein. The horse you are riding needs to enjoy his work (you can tell that I am no dressage rider), needs to have a generous share in the business in hand: I have tried to apply this principle throughout life... especially when soldiering, the whole point of which is training men to eschew their instincts, and to do so willingly. It used to be called leadership: I don't know what they call it now, but horses teach it.

AFTER a couple of years as an armoured car troop leader with my regiment in Germany, I was sent home for a spell of duty with what was then called the Boy's Squadron. It was where young recruits for the Royal Armoured Corps got their first military training, at Bovington Camp, barely 16 miles, as the crow flies, from this house. As military posting go, it was a great stroke of luck.

We worked school terms, and since I didn't own a car I would ride to and from home for my leaves, and sometimes at weekends. In those days, the late 1950s' it seemed a fairly natural thing to do, the great challenge being to get from the south to the north of the county, or vice versa, using the minimum of road, to save the horse's shoes.

During my first, and, as it was to prove only summer leave from Bovington, my father and I rode down to Exmoor and back, taking three days coming and going, stopping overnight wherever there might be a pub with stabling, or an orchard where we could turn the horses out.

It was a great adventure, or it seemed so at the time, and I had my introduction to stag-hunting, both on Exmoor and in the Quantocks. The idea was for my father to do a bit of painting on the moor, and for us both to get our horses fit for the coming hunting season.

That season proved to be an illusion however, as I was suddenly summoned back by my regiment for service in Aden and the Persian Gulf. But it was at that time that my father put Ronald Good's *The Old Roads of Dorset* into my hands, and I became fascinated, obsessed you might perhaps be thinking, with trying to track and piece together some of the old routes that criss-cross the map of Dorset like the wrinkles in an ancient palm – a palm in which so much of the history of the county can be read.

This at least is a taste that I share with Thomas Hardy, so many of whose stories open on a road. *The Mayor of Casterbridge* for instance, starts, God help us, on the A303, at 'Weydon-Priors', Weyhill, just this side of Andover – that's a thought to sooth the mind as one sits in a traffic jam on that hellish road today.

The Return of the Native, as I write being beautifully acted weekly on the wireless, starts with a detailed, in fact rather laboured, typically cod-scholarly, description of the old road that crosses 'Egdon', ie Winfrith Heath.

We have already visited the opening scene of *The Woodlanders*, which is set on the old coach road that runs close by this house. And much of the crucial action of *Tess*, as well as the beginning of the story, takes place on a road, or on the ancient ridgeway that I can see from my attic crow's nest as I write. Hardy teaches us to see old roads as doorways into romance, history and imagination: I go along with that.

THE first horse that I ever bought cost me and a fellow subaltern £15. She was one of batch that had been liberated from the German army stud at Mecklenhorst at the end of the war. They were not allowed to leave the country, and were passed from hand to hand between different owners for that standard sum. She was a Trakhener, an East Prussian breed of great toughness and quality, and we had a lot of fun with her at hunter trials and show jumping.

My last, and best purchase cost me a good slice of the bounty the army gave me when I quit the service. But no horses have given me more pleasure, nor taught me more, than the two we have now, that we bred, backed and broke-in ourselves. 'Making' horses, as well as being my own groom, is something I came to late in life, it has been an unlooked for joy.

Horses, as I believe, don't have that poor thing that we call a memory, they forget nothing. They are not unforgiving, but their trust is not to be trifled with, and, although they are such a strange mixture of rough and gentle, horseplay being no joke for us feeble humans, their soft, so expressive, lambent eye gives the clue, gentleness is the only way with them.

I have come to believe that voice, more than any other thing, is the best means of telling a horse what you want it to do, voice and I suppose body-language – Dandy and Bella both well understand the raised or shaken finger. When I bring them in from grass, often, if they are in placid mood, I lead them negligently at the full length of their ropes, as if they were the last two, unsold, of a bunch of balloons bobbing along gently behind me, except that I talk to them constantly, as possibly one wouldn't talk to a balloon.

And as the three of us thread the wicket out of the paddock, and I juggle them through the stable door, which only admits one of us at a time, and slip their head-collars as they make for the breakfast in their mangers, I feel an enormous sense of pleasure and of achievement that I can manage them, great hulking potentially dangerous brutes and gentle creatures that they are.

Those two horses, and the small herd that has trooped in ones and twos through my life before them, giving me their trust and lending me their courage, have been something beyond price.

I DON'T know how many hours, days or weeks even I must have spent sitting on the mounting block whilst the horses are being shod.

Duffy Fox, our present farrier, has been with us now for years, I dread the day when he finally finds the work too heavy – there can't be much harder outside work than shoeing horses. But no one is more crucial to the smooth running of a stable and keeping a sound string than the farrier, and, most lameness being in the foot, your farrier is nearly always first call before the vet.

Lately a sergeant in the 15th/19th King's Royal Hussars – we both now owe allegiance to the Light Dragoons – Duffy is a man after my own heart. For a start, as an old soldier, it is his habit to say what he means, and to mean what he says, and is totally reliable – I never lost a day's hunting on his account. Secondly, we find the same sorts of things amusing, the more so now that they mostly involve forbidden utterances, thoughts even that are outside the law.

He comes of a family that, in Shakespeare's words, has "done the state some service". His father, born of an English mother, in Belfast, was raised in Tipperary, one of 13 or 14 siblings, Duffy is not sure of the exact total. He volunteered for service in the British army in the Second World War, joining the 15/19H; two other brothers saw war service with the Green Howards; three sisters served with the ATS. Duffy's Uncle Paddy, who joined the 19/19H after the war, is now a Chelsea Pensioner.

Duffy himself, his family having settled in Yorkshire, having endured a lecture from his Headmaster about the importance of staying on in school, bicycled off to the Recruiting Office and enlisted in the Green Howards as a boy soldier, to train as a drummer in the band, although he soon gave up the drumstick for a rifle.

In due course, he transferred into his father's old regiment, and, again in due course, found himself employed in the regimental stables. There he served the rest of his time, a full regular career to twenty-two years, only quitting the stables temporarily when the Regiment went to Ireland. He became a crack shot, representing his regiment at Bisley, is a keen musician, and a family man.

You may guess that Duffy and I have plenty to talk about, as he trims Bella's feet, makes Dandy's shoes, quenches them, and so skilfully nails them on. Going as he does, from yard to yard, he is a great source of news, as well as entertainment. He comes to us faithfully, always just 'five minutes before the published time of parade', every few weeks through the year. We have lots of laughs, Duffy and I: what is more, the horses stay sound and, even in this deep Dorset vale, Dandy keeps his shoes.

DUNGEON, from Donjon, as the Normans called it, after the great Iron Age fortification on its summit, is the hill that stands above this house. A northern outpost of the downland, marooned in the Blackmore Vale, I think of it as the dot under the exclamation mark of the Heights that make such a bold statement on our southern skyline. We ride up there two or three times a week. Perhaps more than anything, that hill, and my familiarity with it, accounts for my being so deeply rooted in this place.

There are a couple of bridle paths one can follow, but, thanks to the generosity of neighbours, we have the freedom of the hill and can go more or less where we please. I was on my own and riding Bella on a particular summer morning that I remember, and decided, since I had a letter to deliver at the Manor House, to take the hill clockwise.

Soon we were off the road and in a field called Park, above the manor. If you can bear another stanza of execrable verse, here is what I said about it at our Village Entertainment:

> *Where did they live, all those years ago?*
> *I've studied this and think I know.*
> *Above where the Manor stands today –*
> *You can walk close by, it's a right of way –*
> *Straddled by three oaks, a chestnut tree,*
> *And an ancient ash, you can clearly see*
> *Still etched square on the ground,*
> *What was once a fortified compound.*
> *That, I have very little doubt,*
> *Is where those de Glanvilles first hung out.*

That old pollard ash is one of my very favourite trees. It is completely hollowed out, just half a husk of a trunk, with stunted and torn stumps of limbs. A real Arthur Rackham tree, it somehow clings on to life, year after year reaching out claws of new growth. Goodness only knows how old it is, and what scenes it has been witness to.

LEAVING the manor ground behind us we climb a steep meadow called Whitedown; a name that tells us, as our village history confirms, that it used once to be ploughed – it's solid chalk beneath the now long established turf, and must have stood out very white above the village. It's a gorgeous flower meadow, jewelled through spring and summer, and, in winter, often alive with flocks of assorted finches, there to rob the seedheads.

As we rise the hill an astonishing panorama comes gradually into view, a complete circle almost, from the Dorsetshire Gap – an ancient entrance to the Heights – by Bulbarrow, right out across the vale to Shaftesbury and the edge of Salisbury Plain. North you can see Stourhead and Alfred's Tower, and west almost to the Brendons and, beyond, only in the mind's eye perhaps, Exmoor. In the middle distance west, over 10 miles away, beyond Halstock, the tump of Pen Hill stands out, to its left the pines at Winyard's Gap, and then, sweeping towards you, the grand arpeggio of the Heights, Telagraph Hill, High Stoy, Dogbury and Ridge Hill.

A pair of ash trees, grown out V-shaped from stumps in the bank of a long abandoned hedge, guards a gateway. You can see those familiar trees from many points on the distant surrounding skyline, they are my homing landmark, as I return, maybe from hunting down west, or as I drop off Salisbury Plain after a day polo-watching in the Home Counties.

Soon we are under the shelter of the great beeches that crown the hill and its earthworks, some of them giants still, some gale-ravaged wrecks, drop the hill, and make for home.

I WONDER if you are familiar with that extraordinary sight, a horse scratching its head with its hind foot – and if you are not, whether I can adequately describe it? An improbable contortion, at the same time somehow delicate and elephantine, balletic yet grotesque, it is almost as though the extended hoof holds out for sipping, in ever so gentile a fashion, a bone-china cup of Earl Grey tea. It is enough to make you laugh out loud, unless, whilst this pantomime is going on, you happen to be in the saddle.

Bella, with her thin skin and skittish ways, is particularly sensitive to flies – clegs madden her, and there is no peace to be had when she feels one on her, all else must go by the board until she should be free of it. The best thing I find is to keep her briskly on the move, and to get through gates as urgently as their sometimes Heath Robinson entanglements allow – I seem to be the only person hereabouts who can hang a gate so that it opens sweetly and closes on the swing.

As we were finally coming off Dungeon, headed for home, and on the road, she dropped anchor with disconcerting suddenness, and went into the rollmop, milking-stool mode, balancing on three legs as she reached forward with her near-hind hoof to dislodge a horsefly from the cleft beneath her jaw.

I held my breath, motionless, above all not wishing to disturb her so precarious poise. But then my horrified eye saw that her extended hoof had actually passed inside the loop of the rein, slackened by her extreme flexion, and that in a second we might both be in a heap on the ungiving tarmac.

Picture it! What an obscure and unlikely accident, a horse catching a hind leg in its reins: what a joke, provided that both survive unhurt: what a story to dine out on! The moment passed. Ever so delicately, as though aware of exactly what she was doing, she safely resumed all fours and we walked quietly home. So much for the virtues of the loose rein.

WINTER MEMORIES

LIKE Arthur Ransome's children who "...didn't mean to go to sea", I never meant to be a Hunting Correspondent. When the job was first offered me by the now Editor of *Country Life* I turned it down. Like many who ride to hounds I knew shamefully little about venery – too busy managing my horse and getting across the country in one piece – I didn't reckon I rode well enough for visiting, let alone for public inspection. And anyway it seemed a rather foolish enterprise for someone already in his sixtieth year

I was down with 'flu, and in an enfeebled state, when Clive Aslet had the generosity to repeat the offer. Hounds were due to meet nearby, and I weakly said that I would give it a go. What tipped the balance was that I had at that time my 'horse of a lifetime', a great leonine chestnut giant by the famous Irish Draft sire Prince of Diamonds. He was what we call a 'vale' horse, that is to say he had the athleticism and courage to carry even the most inept rider across our formidable Dorset vale. His name was Woody, and you may read of some of his exploits in the pages that follow.

Woody gave me the confidence to go visiting. The kindness and encouragement that I met with on those early forays emboldened me to venture further a-field, and to ride whatever horse hunts might generously provide for me. And the patience of huntsmen, with whom in the early days I spent as much time as I could in kennels and in covert, taught me to take a more intelligent interest in hounds. Under their guidance, and with a lot of help from more knowledgeable friends, I began to write about the real business of hunting with a new assurance.

So started a career I never dreamed of, which goes on to this day, despite my twice firmly deciding to retire.

1991/92 - GETTING STARTED
South Dorset — Seavington

WHATEVER anyone else may think, your own hunt, like your own village, regiment or whatever, is incomparable. But in sober truth there really cannot be many hunting countries to match the scrap of vale where the South Dorset Hunt meet on alternate Tuesdays until the end of January. Centred on Dungeon, the hill above this house, it is a dairy-farming area peppered with small villages with important-sounding names. But the heavy going, and the tremendous, often double-ditched,

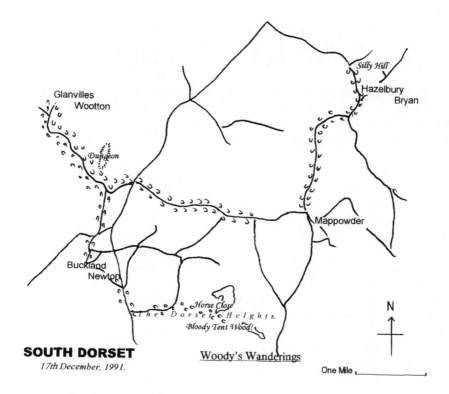

SOUTH DORSET

17th December, 1991.

Woody's Wanderings

One Mile

N

hedges make it a most challenging country in which to follow hounds.

When I was a boy we used to 'bank' the hedges. You could get anywhere on a clever pony such as the one my sister and I had, up out of the clinging clay over a ditch, scramble somehow through the cut-and-laid hedge on the bank top, and down, probably over another ditch on the landing side. But today, with the hedges mechanically cut, *en brosse*, there's no foothold, you have to fly the lot... or find a gate. Only an athletic horse with a good heart will do for the Dorset vale. My old horse Woody, now long retired, had nerve and skill enough for both of us, and was in his prime when I made this, my first foray as a hunting correspondent.

It was just before Christmas. After a week of fog and frosts the forecast was for a wet, unsettled day. The temperature was high for December, the wind in the southwest, and the glass steady. Smoke was fleeing chimneys, heavy clouds dragged their skirts across the Dorset Heights to our south, and the wind threw the occasional spattering of rain in our faces, as Woody and I hacked the four miles to the meet near Mappowder. Whatever the weather there cannot be many better feelings than setting out from home to hunt in the next parish.

It was a busy morning, plenty of foxes, scent catchy. But we had covered a lot of ground, jumped a few respectable hedges and had various adventures, when, after a three mile point, we ran a fox to ground in a grass drove by a place called Silly Hill, well into the neighbouring Blackmore and Sparkford Vale country. The mood was happy as we hacked back through Hazlebury Bryan into our own country. Second horses were taken by the lucky few, and Edward Knowles, our young huntsman, set about looking for another fox.

THE temperature had dropped and the promised wind was rising, throwing the odd handful of rain at us, when a hedgerow fox was found and hounds got off almost on his brush. He took a quick circuit in the vale, and then headed for the hills, hounds giving a wonderful and helpful cry.

The obstacle that immediately faced us was a large hedge by any standards, bringing down the first three or four who bravely tackled it. In the fraction of a doubtful pause that followed I fancied that I heard the hounds well to our left, and running, in the opposite direction. It is convenient to have such fancies when the way forward is uninviting, but, just for once, fancy proved correct.

Catching a gate before the damage stewards shut it, and hopping a few familiar rails, Woody and I made Horse Close – 40 acres of bog and woodland – just after hounds had entered it, and were joined by the Huntsman, and the only two members of the field to survive the monster hedge. Hounds crashed on, forcing their fox out of the cover, up the steep slope of the downland escarpment at the vale's edge, and into the wood above. The pace was terrific.

We straggled, the Huntsman going on, we doing our best to help him forward and seeing to the gates. Suddenly, I am not sure quite how, in a place oddly and memorably called Bloody Tent Wood, a locked wicket divided Edward from his hounds, and me from my companions. He climbed the gate, and we picked our way gingerly down to where by then hounds were marking at an enormous badger set. And that is how, completely undeserved, out of a field of thrusters, Woody and I ended a good thing in the South Dorset vale alone with hounds.

The day was not finished, but we were. The first hard surface told of a loose shoe: I turned for home. A gale was getting up, and the occasional dash of heavier rain suggested such haste as was decent with a tired, deserving horse. Five miles to go and the light just failing, it could have been any Christmas holiday since childhood. Woody was no doubt thinking of his manger: I had a story in my head, and a song in my heart. I was hooked.

BOXING DAY

WHATEVER grownups may think about it, children adore hunting on Boxing Day. I remember thinking of little else during the Michaelmas term at school other than whether or not "saucer-eyes" would be out – she who was in my ride at Pony Club camp – whether she would remember me, whether or not my parents would let me have a velvet cap instead of that awful unromantic "square" bowler, and if my sister (who's pictures illustrate these pages) would let me ride Punch, who jumped, or make me take Bob, who didn't.

The uncertainties did not stop with the arrival of the longed-for holidays. Could we get the clippers repaired when they broke with the ponies only half done, would the farrier come, as he promised, early on Christmas Day to replace the shoe lost on Christmas Eve – (Why oh why did I go for that extra day)? Worst of all, would those idiotic London cousins get the "White Christmas" they were for ever going on about, and which equally idiotic weather forecasters seemed to think we all yearned for?

Christmas Day itself barely registered. Until you actually got to the meet the whole thing was total agony, ten to one "saucer eyes" had a cold, or was sick or something and wasn't out.

WE ALWAYS had a favourite uncle and aunt down for Christmas. A city stockbroker, my uncle had been a great hunting man in his youth, but he just had the one day a year at the time I remember, and how painful that single day must have been!

My father would hire a horse for him, and it was always a great excitement to find out what sort of nag he had managed to dredge up when every decent local horse was already spoken for.

My sister and I would ride and lead the 10 miles by bridleways to the meet, two ponies and two horses, and think nothing of it – that perhaps is the only difference from later years.

We would come off the old downland track at the place where we park the horseboxes today, and, depending on the time, jog or saunter the last mile by road to the small rural Dorset town that was Thomas Hardy's Weatherbury, and where the meet has been for as long as anyone could remember.

With every converging road and lane jammed full with hastening people, on foot, on horseback, or in cars, we would turn in at the great iron gates where, either side, familiar figures collect the one 'cap', for the hunt staff, that no-one grudges, and join what would look like a part of Epsom

Downs on Derby Day.

Where did they come from, those crowds on Boxing Day, the teeming riders, most of whom would be home for lunch, and the throng on foot? Town visits country, and both turn out to hunt, and do it every year.

The Hunt's regular followers would be on parade in strength, they and their horses as smart as could be, but almost as many again would be visitors, one-timers, children having their first day, old men their last, many, like my Uncle Matthew, having their annual day.

Anxiety, adventure, excitement; fringes and curls in all the wrong places, plaits, pig-tails, pony-tails, ear-rings, drawing room make-up, bulbous bottoms, bursting buttons on borrowed coats, bad boots, worse whips, disastrous ties with dazzling pins, harlequin browbands, circus ponies, gypsy ponies, every colour of tail ribbon. Enthusiasm excuses all – except a kick.

On foot would be jaded parents, liverish uncles, raffish aunts, curious cousins, and seemingly countless children weaving in and out of one's pony's fetlocks, bedecked with the spoils of Christmas stockings, bobble hats and other garish gear.

Meanwhile drinks would circulate, those who were perhaps not meant to get them, get them, blood-alcohol levels recover, jollity spreads.

As we at last move off, people clap a little, and, when our Field Master leads the colourful cavalcade out of the grand iron gates again and into the main street… yes there is a cheer.

Another Boxing Day meet is over – but whatever became of "saucer-eyes"?

ON MY second outing I set off westward with Woody and the horsebox in fulfilment of an old ambition: my parents had hunted with the Seavington before the Second World War, and I had long wanted to see that childhood fabled hunt for myself. We were to meet at a splendid country house and Wildlife Park, Cricket St Thomas, and were bidden there for tea, and, as the weather looked set fair, the day promised well. In fact I was to have my first experience of the hunting correspondent's nightmare – a blank day.

My enthusiasm was somewhat checked when, as we cleared Yeovil, my wandering eye lighted on an empty heel: my spurs it seemed were still hanging on the whip rack in the hall at home. And when I later climbed on Woody, and it was patently too late to put things right, I discovered that the French rein with its ridged grips (Woody was iron-mouthed), which should have been attached to the curb bit, was innocuously attached to the bridoon on his double bridle.

So, through pure carelessness, on this my first professional foray, I would have cast myself adrift in foreign waters without benefit of either screw or anchor. Woody, it seemed, was to be even more firmly in command of things than usual. Spurs I borrowed from Cricket's chatelaine, an old friend; the curb, as it turned out, I hardly needed... until the very end of the day.

JUST as a bridge hand with tens in it, however disgusting to pick up, cannot properly be called a Yarborough, so a day when foxes are found cannot properly be called blank. We did find foxes, but the scent was negligible. I felt for the huntsman, Peter Collins, who naturally wanted to show what his hounds could do, and who worked as hard as a man could with the materials available, but was not rewarded.

When we finally turned for home, and re-entered Cricket's parkland, it was a sight to see the knots of riders descending the sides of the grass amphitheatre in which the great house, setting for the popular TV series *To The Manor Born*, stands. Our way took us past the animal pens.

Woody, who had seemed to think nothing of Bactrian camels encountered in the morning, and now appeared quite unflustered by a pair of demoiselle cranes and a flock of flamingos, was electrified when we finally passed a family of elephants, one of which improved the occasion with a jungle squeal. He bolted, and we reached the horsebox in a state of barely suppressed equine hysteria. So ended my first hunting engagement away from home.

1992/93 – BRANCHING OUT
Nantcol Valley – Eggesford – Huckworthy Bassets – Pembrokeshire – Villers-Cotterêts

MY FIRST full season took me twice to Wales, twice out with foot packs, and finally to France. It also gave me my first, nervous, taste of what was to become almost the greatest pleasure of the work, riding other people's well-schooled horses – and I took my first fall.

FELL hunts wage a form of warfare against the mountain fox. More than once during my day with the Nantcol Valley hounds, in Snowdonia, images came back to me from the distant past of infantry-training at Sandhurst as, like a handful of partisans, we negotiated scree, bog, torrent and steep hillside, sometimes in sunlight, sometimes in a blinding squall. Fell hunting, I discovered, is an earnest affair, with no frills, its purpose being the control of foxes in the defence of the hill farmer's livelihood. The fell hunter is to the follower of a smart lowland pack as the guerrilla is to the guardsman.

In the fells, foxes prey on lambs from rock earths, locally called borrans, high up the mountain: the effects can be devastating to small farmers. These rock piles are everywhere, and injury from falling boulders is not unknown.

The method of hunting hill foxes, which is far older than modern methods of lowland foxhunting, consists in an early start, hounds drawing a likely area for the fox's overnight 'drag' at the mountain foot, following this to his temporary resting place or 'lair', probably some way up the mountain side, then "un-kennelling" and hunting him. This was how John Peel operated – you may perhaps have already been getting echoes of that famous hunting song?

Fell hounds are smaller and lighter than normal foxhounds, with which there is some careful interbreeding. The typical fell hound is built on a different scale, and its feet – hare-shaped rather than cat-shaped – are designed to survive prolonged work on rock. It also has a characteristic pendulous ear, which would be nothing but a nuisance in close cover and pushing through thorn hedges, but which has its uses on the mountain. I was to envy the hounds this feature when we were caught by a storm on the exposed top of Llawlech, and I tried ineffectually to pull the crown of my cloth cap over my windward ear.

WE MET at 7.30am, at the kennels, inland from Harlech, a scene of great noise and activity. The woeful baying of the handful of hounds sentenced to be left behind; terriers, not yet coupled, all over the place; and the pack vociferously demanding to be loaded; all suggested urgency. We were soon off for the mountain, a convoy of three cars only, led by the hound van.

It had been a wild night. An old ash had disobligingly shed an enormous limb on the only access track, so we took to our feet a mile or so earlier than planned, but hounds were drawing by a tarn on the south side of Moelfre by about nine, and found shortly after, high up the side of the long ridge of Llawlech. First hunting a drag, then the un-kennelled fox, they were following the 500-metre contour, or thereabouts.

As is usual, the whipper-in kept with or above the pack, whilst we kept abreast of them at the bottom of the rising valley, assaulting the face of the hill only when the pack had disappeared over its crest. This proved to be a steep climb by any standards. Pausing to catch breath, and looking behind me, I could see a storm beating towards us across Cardigan Bay. Strands of rain from dark, low clouds were bombarding the surface of the sea. Clearly we were in for it.

At the summit of the ridge we met the first of many walls. More than six feet high, stoutly built of dry stone, goodness knows when or by whom, it took some climbing, and the drop on the far side was not invit-ing. However, with its generous lee it was to prove a friend when the storm hit us. The wind was terrific, a dense cloud settled like an enormous tea cosy over the entire scene, and the hounds were lost.

WHEN the cloud lifted, a distant cry directed us to the northern shoulder of Llawlech, and, after a long descending traverse of the rock-strewn mountain- side, we rejoined the pack, marking at a chaos of boulders, a typical and well-known rock earth.

We spent half an hour fruitlessly trying to dislodge this first fox, and then set off to explore the possibilities of an uninviting crag-cum-hill called Craig y Dinas. Our route took us along an old drovers' way, paved with giant slabs of rock. Drawing loose rock and scree on the west face of the feature hounds marked their second fox, but again we were defeated by the labyrinthine nature of the place. A third fox was then found, vig-orously hunted, and killed above ground; and so the day went on.

As well as watching the hounds work, and admiring the skill of Alan Owen who was hunting them, who, even in totally blind conditions, seemed to know exactly where they were, I had got a lot of fun from the antics of the terriers. All except one, Cymro, seventeen-years old and Alan's favourite, they were in couples, save when required to work. They ran like quicksilver everywhere, and although the tumbles, jerks and general frustration of their enforced pairing aroused my compassion, my lasting memory was of the happiest group of small dogs I had ever seen.

Driving up from Dorset I had been playing a tape of reminiscences of hunting with the Pytchley in the great days between the wars, regretful of times that can never return, of hunting with a glamour and on a scale impossible, even if desirable today. There had been just nine of us out fol-lowing the Nantcol Valley on this, my first day fell hunting.

MY FIRST outing with the Eggesford, in Devon, was a memorable one, not least because I was invited to attach myself to the coat tails of the Huntsman, Paul Larby. It was also my first experience of being mounted by my hosts: I was to ride no fewer than three horses that day – well two-and-a-half to be truthful, my third ride was a pony.

I don't in the least mind being called a hero, but people are very wide of the mark when they say how brave I must be, riding strange horses in strange hunting countries. I did have a few butterflies fluttering around in my tummy as I drove west that day, but it was to be the last time that I was to suffer that sort of insect trouble.

Hunts want their visitor to enjoy his day and mount him accordingly: I know no better feeling than climbing on a horse that tells you by its body language straight away that it thoroughly understands its business, and enormously enjoys it. Just such a horse was Whisky, my first borrowed mount – "leave her head alone" her owner cautioned, that was music to my ears; and when Whisky lost a shoe one of the masters, promptly and very generously handed me his horse Liquorish; and when Liquorish lost a shoe, and I thought that my day was truly over, a pony called Lucket was conjured up from nowhere. It was a very happy, reassuring day.

I HAD never followed bassets before my day with the Huckworthy, who used to hunt the old Blackmore Vale country on the Somerset/Dorset border, but, along with their cofounder, Audrey Parlby, are today sadly no more. But many years before, when exercising an indifferent point-to-point horse in the fog somewhere in Yorkshire, preparing no doubt to make a fool of myself again on the following Saturday, I was suddenly aware of strange music, a sort of warbling, church bell sound.

Through the hedge burst a small pack of basset hounds in full cry, a string of them, each little chap with his nose close to the ground, but ever and anon throwing his tongue. They crossed my vision and disappeared into the murk, their sound dying like that of swans flying overhead, and not a man with them.

The Huckworthy broke this old dream-like memory. It was a pleasure to be close to those eager little hounds, a joy to watch them work, and of great interest to compare their way of hunting with that of foxhounds. In a sense, bassets do not hunt as a pack, for each individual must work the line for himself it seemed, and each confirm it with his own voice, as they would jostle and shoulder each other in their keenness to own it.

MY DAY with the Pembrokeshire was to be similarly hound-centred, although I was extremely well-mounted, on an event horse, had my first, as it were, professional fall – the horse came down with me on Severn shore, ruining my sandwiches – and we did a fair amount of jumping.

We had stayed over-night, I was able for the first time to see a huntsman, in this case Gary Barber, draw his pack for the next day's hunting, and to fix in my mind the identity of some of his star hounds, notably Craftsman and Cricketer.

Drawing the pack recalled uneasy memories of hopelessly waiting to be picked for this or that scratch team in the gym at school. The hounds undoubtedly knew what was going on, but I suspected that their feelings about being selected were a touch ambivalent: those not drawn went straight through to the noisome dining room next door, those picked went hungry.

It was not to be an easy day for Gary, foxes were difficult to find, scent poor. The first fox, found after drawing for more than an hour was soon lost, but then, sometime later Craftsman spoke to a second fox, in a hedge, close by me, and a wonderful deep voice he had … and somewhere near three o'clock a hound spoke to our third fox. I was with Gary at the time, all of a hundred yards away; without a second's hesitation, "Hark to Cricketer!" he cried, and away we went full pelt.

I left Pembrokeshire, the Welsh daffodils showing and the end of my first full season all too clearly in sight, feeling that I was beginning to learn my new trade, and with the dawning of an immense respect for the skill and character of the professional huntsman.

THERE is a pocket tape-recorder on my desk that I used to carry when I started to write about hunting. I sometimes play one particular old tape on it to myself. It takes me back to a vast stretch of ancient forest the other side of Paris where Diana and I first went staghunting. What I listen for is the unforgettable and dreamlike sound of the horn music, horn answering horn down those seemingly endless glades and rides, as they have over the centuries in that great medieval royal hunting forest.

Diana never normally came with me on my hunting expeditions, I would worry too much about her, and the job might get neglected – besides, who would have looked after our horses at home? But this was one occasion too good for her to miss, and we did nearly miss it, due to diverting on our journey via Maison Chanel, and almost getting trapped for ever in the Paris traffic.

However, one hyper-expensive handbag, endless 'croissant' manoeuvres on the *Boulevard Périphérique*, and several near-heart-attacks later, we made our rendezvous with hounds, the hunt, and a pair of hirelings that looked more like toast-racks than hunters. "Quel est le nom de ce cheval?" I asked the groom, and was rewarded with a mountainous Gallic shrug, either at my fractured pronunciation, or at the idiocy of the question, the first I always ask.

The French are not as sentimental as we are about animals. It was perhaps just as well that we were late, and there was not much time to study our mounts, or Diana might have got no further. In fact both horses, despite their starveacre appearance, proved to be as fit as fleas, were unbelievably sure-footed, carried us to perfection, and seemed to thoroughly enjoy their work, but they just did not own an ounce of spare flesh between them.

There was barely time, before the hurly-burly started, to take in the splendid and stylish dress of the mounted field. Bright blue frock coats with silver lace and swords were worn by the men, and knee-boots – very sensible when you are galloping all day among trees – side-saddle and three-cornered hats for the ladies. Just about every other mounted follower carried, over the shoulder like a bandolier, a great convoluted shiny brass hunting horn.

The *Trompe de Chasse* is used, not as the English hunting horn is, to command the hounds, but to rally and inform the field, to tell everyone, scattered as we were soon to be, through the dark endless labyrinth of the forest, how the hunt was progressing. Each call, often rehearsed, skilfully played, telling its own tale to those who knew the music, from *L'attaque* (the find) to the *Hallali*, when the stag is finally taken, ever drawing the field on in the right direction.

HOW WE went that day! Three hours we went non-stop, belting helter-skelter up rides, across clearings, or through standing timber, often over the most atrocious going. Always straining for the fleeting music of the pack, ever hoping for clues from the helpful horns of those in contact with the hounds or quarry.

At one place we suddenly burst upon a fairy-tale chateau, in another clattered through a beautiful farmyard. But mostly we were in the depths of the forest, with the feeling that our small group might have been absolutely alone with the hunted stag and hounds, in a tapestry of music. It was unforgettable.

At last the stag broke into the open, stood at bay in a field of young corn, a shot rang out, and the hunt was over. The *Curée*, the ceremony of the rewarding of the hounds, followed, and there was a concert of fanfares by the assembled and now dismounted horn-players. Champagne at the kennels, and later more bubbly and a hunt dinner completed a memorable day.

A mounted trophy, presented to Diana, and hanging in our hall, and a certain very smart evening bag, remind me of our short French hunting holiday. But what lives most with me is the music of those horns, echoing down the ages from a thousand years before we British learnt our love of hunting from the French.

1993/1994
Berkeley — Border — Dumfriesshire — Exmoor — South Dorset
Blackmore & Sparkford Vale — Fell Festival

"WE'RE expecting 200 antis, and your horse has a poisoned foot" was the unwelcome message to arrive a couple of days before I was due to go at short notice to the Berkeley, to write up their opening meet. There was nothing for it but to take Woody, thus breaking a firm rule for self-preservation that I had already made, of always riding a local horse.

The prospect of antis didn't trouble me, but they have 'rhines' in the Berkeley country, great arms of the sea — well, arms of the Severn — and you need a horse that knows how to jump them.

I was frankly scared as I drove up to Gloucestershire that Friday evening, scared of making a fool of myself, scared also of the social side of it, I am happiest hunting with farmers — it was my first visit to a 'grand' hunt - but we got away with it, Woody and I. He had presence enough for both of us, and neither 'rhine' nor anti did we encounter.

NEXT came a real treat, my first visit to the Borders, where I was to return again and again, whenever I could persuade various Editors that they needed news of hunting in those parts. I shall save for later a description of one of my several outings with Michael Hedley's Border hounds, but, on this first occasion, I went on from them for a day with Sir Rupert Buchanan-Jardine's unique, now sadly dispersed, black-and-tan hounds.

I first met them in the hunt kennels, then at Milk Castle, and was astonished by their size and physique, one almost knocked me down in the enthusiasm of its greeting. They were equally striking from the back of a horse, when we met, in a gale, next morning. But most memorable of all was the deep, sonorous and unforgettable tumult of their cry, when they eventually found a fox after a long sodden, blank, apologetic hour.

It is very difficult I find to parry the apologies of one's hosts about the weather, or at the failure to find a fox – especially as I always half feel that it is my fault, that I am a Jonah, and that hounds would immediately find and the weather improve if I were to go home.

However find a fox they did, and we had a lovely hunt, touching places with magic names, such as Water of Milk, Hungry Hill, Nutholm, Bowmillholm, Sorrysite Moor and Banksideyett. Yett, I had learned only two days before on the other side of Scotland, means gate: I was learning quite a lot in my travels…. and enjoying them enormously.

DURING the previous summer I had had the great good luck to meet Captain Ronnie Wallace, when he was judging at a Puppy Show. I literally sat at his feet, on the grass, being told what was what whilst we had tea – I metaphorically sat at his feet thereafter. For, from that day, that remarkable man befriended me.

I seldom, from then on, made up my winter schedule without his advice – it is so important not to visit hunts that are temporarily for whatever reason in the doldrums – and he encouraged me to consult him at will, which, with a great deal of screwing up of courage, I used to do.

An invitation to stay, and to hunt with his hounds, followed our meeting, and found me, around Christmas, seeking out Mounsey Farm, above Dulverton, which was to become quite a familiar destination for me.

It was an amazing sight to see the Captain, mounted, surrounded by his hounds – I have a picture of it in front of me as I write – every hound has its eyes on him. It was wonderful to witness how he controlled the pack, in silence: I never heard his horn or voice that morning, until 1pm. And it was a parable to watch how he got about the moor, like a general on a battlefield, moving with no more haste that was absolutely necessary, directly, from each spot where he was needed to the next.

When I sent him my report by fax that evening, for his correction and approval, I had written "Throughout all that long hunt I seldom saw him do more than walk his horse". His only comment was, "David, would you awfully mind changing that word 'walk' to trot?". I came to have a prodigious respect and liking for that man.

IF I HAVE set you wondering, that, before filing it, I should check out my 'copy' with the Captain, I must tell you that it was, still is, my invariable practice to get my report approved by the host hunt. I can't think of anything stupider than a visitor pretending to know more about a day's hunting than the man who hunted hounds, or anything more boring than trying to carry in one's head, when you are wanting to enjoy your day, the exact name of every place and person that needs to be remembered. So, 'relax and check back' has become my motto, my recipe for enjoying, surely the most enjoyable of jobs.

It was at this juncture, towards the end of my third season that, greatly daring, I offered my services to Michael Clayton, the Editor of *Horse & Hound*, hoping that the Editor of *Country Life* wouldn't mind – which, after an initial *froideur*, evidently he didn't. At least, he put up with it for three seasons: I am not sure if anyone had managed to report hunting for both magazines before, I like to think not.

So I finished what had been an extraordinarily wet season with two days sloshing around in our own vale on Woody. One, from this house, with the South Dorset, and one with the neighbouring Blackmore & Sparkford Vale. Neither day was particularly distinguished, both were fun, until the last one ended in disaster.

Faithful old Woody had for some time been a bit dodgy in his feet, with navicular disease, the deterioration of a small bone inside the hoof, caused by his being overworked as a half-grown youngster in Ireland. The discomfort this caused could be controlled for some time by a blood-thinning drug that I called 'powdered banknotes', I forget its proper name.

As the condition worsened I doubled up with judicious, and sometimes injudicious doses of the painkiller 'Bute', which had the effect, if overdone, of rendering Woody unaware of my presence in the saddle, or any attempts I might be making to modify his speed. He still adored his hunting.

Overawed by the prospect of a day with the smart B&SV, with their large, dashing field – a quite different outfit from my own homely South Dorset – and concerned that Woody should not put in a rare refusal, I overdid the 'Bute'. Sometime, about the middle of the day, he took off with me, galloped over a concrete culvert, lost his footing, and came crashing down. He ended up cut all over the place and lame in the shoulder, I was not much better: apart from a day on foot with fell hounds, it put an end to my season.

One of the hard-bitten ladies who follow the B&SV, hearing of my predicament and of its cause said "It serves you right!". It was a fair enough verdict, except that we both recovered, Woody and I, and things could have been a great deal worse.

1994/1995
Devon & Somerset — Seavington — Wilton — Portman - Tedworth

WOODY carried me for all except the first of my outings in a season, in which, as you can see, I did not venture far afield, and which perhaps we might skip lightly over. But you need to meet Lucy, a grey mare, very generously lent me by her Belgian owner, which I rode on my visit to the D&S Staghounds, have ridden on Exmoor and the Quantocks often since, and still am lucky enough to ride today, ten seasons later. Here is a rather fanciful account of an adventure we once had on one of our many outings together. I call the piece 'Bewitched, bothered and bewildered'.

WE SAW the stag away, Lucy and I. It had just one horn and, I can tell you that, as the day wore on and we seemed to become more and more be-witched, I wondered if it wasn't in fact a unicorn we were hunting.

Lucy's owner had said "I wouldn't follow me today", so I fixed on what must have been the oldest bowler hat in the world, mounted on a confidential-looking, cobbish roan for my pilot. Thought I to myself, "No nonsense there, he looks as if he knows his way around, and Lucy will have the legs on him".

The stag took a couple of leisurely circuits of the hilltop, and then flung off like a bolas into the vale, with the bitch pack after him, lickerty-split. It was bound to be a road hunt for the field, once we were off the hill and, do what I might, the roan cob trotted clean away from us: I durst not canter on a borrowed horse on tarmac.

Have you ever been completely lost out hunting, on your own, in a strange and empty country? And then suddenly realised, as I then did, that you have no money on you, cannot remember for the moment what was said about getting home, or work out in which direction that home lies, and then noticed that the sun is dropping? There is only one thing for it – find hounds.

Lucy and I pressed on, for more than an hour, following doubtful white scrapings on the tarmac. Up a stream bed we went at one time, along a horribly narrow and high tow-path at another. Two Land Rovers passed us, both as lost as we.

A "holloa" turned into a train rushing by in an unseen cutting. The cry of hounds proved to be only a 'Hebrews Chorus' from the poor wretches left behind in kennel. Do you wonder that I began to feel that I had wandered into fairyland?

The nightmare eventually ended as suddenly as it had begun, when, there, round the corner were my pilot, the rusty bowler, the roan cob, and the surviving remnant of the field. The 'unicorn' had vanished, as unicorns no doubt usually do, and hounds were at a loss.

At that moment, as if it had been waiting on starting blocks in a relay race, a stag with an enormous head of horn lumbered into view, taking the lane ahead of us in-and-out like an eventer. The Huntsman looked a question at the Master, who seemed rather puzzlingly to say "Slight musty smell!", and off we galloped, mercifully across the fields this time.

Do you have a problem as I sometimes do, making out what people say out hunting? It was fully ten minutes later that I realised that what the Master had really said in answer to Richard Down's unspoken query was "Might just as well". It was two hours later, and past 6pm, when we lost that second stag on the top of the Quantocks.

We had gone some 30 miles that day, and there was just one hound on at the end, a lovely toast-coloured bitch called Walnut, both Masters, and just two members of the field... old rusty-bowler on his roan, long-legged Lucy, and me.

"What sort of day did you have?" Diana asked when I eventually got home. "Magic" I replied.

1995/1996 – IN THE THICK OF IT
Wilton – Dummer Beagles – Sinnington – Buccleuch – Huckworthy
Suffolk – South Dorset – Eskdale & Ennerdale
Mendip Farmers – West Somerset – Exmoor – New Forest

"TALLY-HO" squeaked the little girl from the Pony Club, "False alarm!" growled a grown-up, as a brace of hares made off from the maize hounds were drawing. It was just after sunrise, and I was out cub hunting with the Wilton. A Saharan summer had followed two of the wettest winters in memory and, as I was to find in the weeks that followed, scent was almost non-existent, conditions really testing for both hounds and huntsmen.

This was to be our busiest winter. I write in the plural because, whilst I was quartering the country Diana had to run our stable. We were both hunting regularly from home, with two horses 'in', and young stock out at grass. I was with the Dummer, in Gloucestershire, for their opening meet, with the Sinnington, in Yorkshire, on All Soul's Day, and back in Scotland, with the Buccleuch, on Remembrance Day.

Some days, and some horses particularly stick in the mind. I can never forget a wonderful burst we had in the Buccleuch Saturday, in-bye (ie farmed) country. I was, I had learnt over the dinner table, to be mounted on a five-year-old Apaloosa called Monkey, a name that had given me a rather restless night – what tricks would he get up to I wondered. But Monkey was perfection, and the well-fenced grassland on the banks of Ale Water a dream.

In fact everything went swimmingly that season until I was so foolish as to agree to take Woody for 'one last day', the last of many last days, in the South Dorset vale. I knew that the deep going and the big jumps were becoming too much for him, but hounds were meeting here, in our paddock, *Horse & Hound* said "Go on!", and the temptation was too great.

Diana had fractured her collar bone the week before, so I had her wonderful horse, oddly named The Bean, in the morning, then nipped home and picked up Woody, rejoining hounds on Dungeon, above the house. They found just as we arrived, but, as we came out of covert and faced the steep dive down into the vale where in the past he has always joyously carted me, Woody stood rooted, and let the field go from him.

I have never been so clearly spoken to by a horse, nor so wisely. The descent was too much for his poor old feet, and he didn't want to know about those big hedges any more. I was to hunt him, judiciously, in undemanding country, for two further seasons – he would still go over timber like a bird – but, from that moment, the Post Office loomed… for both of us really.

1996/1997
Quantock Staghounds – Border – Braes of Derwent – Puckeridge
South Dorset – Cattistock – Eggesford – Cotley Harriers
Fell Festival – Portman – Crawley & Horsham

I AM conscious of having only told you half a story. No hunting article ever gets into print without pictures. Second only to getting settled happily in the saddle, my great concern at every meet is that the photographer should be there and on time, and that he should be someone who knows hunting, and is sufficiently resourceful and self-sufficient to keep up with hounds. Except for just once, I never had a problem.

The exception was at my very first outing. I had supposed, silly me, that, since I was a complete beginner, *Country Life* would send out some seasoned expert to support my efforts. Not a bit of it, a knock came at the door "Where are the dogs?" my supposed guide and mentor asked. He was a fashion photographer, a veteran of the catwalk, who had never seen a foxhound in his life.

We were to do a lot of work together, Brian Moody and I, and become good friends. On that first day, as it happens, he produced the best action shot of a girl tackling one of our big vale hedges I have ever seen – it 'sold' the article, and in a sense sold me: it appeared under the headline "Derring- do in Dorset".

Since then I must have worked with a couple of dozen different 'snappers', as they are known in the trade. They are pleasant partnerships, renewed here and there from time to time, depending whom the London office send. With *Horse & Hound* Trevor Meeks has become my regular accomplice: I like to think that we are equally glad to see each other at a meet.

WORKING now for a second employer, I was able to return to hunts where I had felt particularly at home such as the Border, the Seavington, the Exmoor and the Eggesford, not to mention the South Dorset. The Eggesford this time mounted me on Mr Christian, the Grand National horse: he was a lovely, snaffle ride, a perfect gentleman: a day on his back was like shaking hands with a VC. In case you will perhaps not be quite so eager as I was for these return visits, I will just tell you of one outing in the 96/97 season, my best hunt in years.

You will perhaps be shocked to learn that Woody was again my partner when I went, by invitation, to the Cattistock; but I asked for a downland day, and I was confident that he would cope. It was a Saturday morning in the Christmas holidays, a great freeze had just relented. We met at Wraxall, and did nothing through a scentless morning.

"The only train of the day on the Weymouth to Bristol line rattled safely by at about 1.30pm" I later wrote, "when the wind, which had started the day in the south-west, shifted to a colder quarter. Suddenly the hounds' music changed from a minor to a major key and we were off."

"They had found their fox just by Chilfrome, in Master's Bog, ran him over Daw's Hill, almost to the meet. They went back over Daw's again, checked among sheep by Lancombe Lane then, beginning to run really well, across the Crewkerne road to Punchbowl Wood, Frogmore Farm, on to Colesmoor, past Ferndown Barn to Wynford Wood. They checked here, then went on across the Eggardon Hill road to Shatcombe Farm, leaving West Compton on our left, and rolled him over in the withy beds just short of the Roman road."

Fifty minutes, fast and furious, and a five mile point, on old turf. Woody was on top form all the way; it was very nearly my last day on him, we did the Portman again together, for *Hound* magazine, and the Cotley – both downland days, on top of the ground – but I reluctantly retired him at the end of the season. He still lives in well-earned retirement, with his stablemate The Bean, to this day.

1997/1998 — CLOUDS GATHER

Minehead Harriers — Barlow —Morpeth — Aldenham Harriers
South & West Wilts — Royal Artillery — Heythrop - Two Bridges Hunt Club

IF YOU have read this far you will not need telling that I am a bit dotty about horses – I don't pretend to ride them especially well, but there is an empathy there which has come to mean a great deal to me.

Being regularly employed as a hunting correspondent has been a bit like being let loose in a sweet shop, quite often, when I cannot sleep at night, I tell over in my mind some of the horses that have been so very kindly found for me by hunts. Rustler, out of Kevin and Ruth Lamacraft's Timberscombe yard, my ride with the Minehead Harriers, often comes to mind.

A great big dark brown, with a split ear, he was a favourite of Captain Wallace's, who had bred him. When, towards the end of a long day, Rustler lost a shoe, Ruth Lamacraft hopped off her horse Sam. Then, when Sid Westcott blew for home, "I hooked a finger round the buckle of the rein, let Sam get on with it, and daydreamed my way home, a happy man".

There was in fact 'trouble at home'. With Woody's retirement our two home-bred youngsters, Dandy and his sister Bella were my regular rides, and it was not as easy as I had hoped it would be, getting them going. Typically of that time, I had started the season late, recovering from a fall, and it was mid-November before I got down to the Minehead Harriers.

Anxious to catch up, I did two days back-to-back, Friday and Saturday, with the Barlow, in Derbyshire, and the Morpeth, in Northumberland. If you know your hunting geography you will realize that those two countries are 150 miles apart. It was a crazy plan, but I guess I was desperate, and it worked. How I managed the nuts and bolts of it, we got soaked on the Friday, let alone the writing – keeping the two days separate in my mind – I cannot remember. Two top-class horses, trouble-free rides, no doubt contributed to my getting away with it.

You will have noticed what year we were in. That Barlow Friday, November 28th, was the day the first anti-hunting bill passed through the House of Commons; I heard news of it on the car radio after hunting. We were already well under the shadow cast by the change of government in the previous May: malign meddling with rural affairs, alternating neglect and bungling of farming and country concerns were to be our lot. Perhaps that was why I was in such a fever to be out on a horse with hounds.

WILLOW, Revel, Rumskill, Detori and Harry were my rides for the remaining engagements of that season, whilst I continued to struggle at home. Dandy was learning and improving, in fact he was earning golden opinions, the farrier, bless him, brought me a story of how someone in the hunt had said how good he looked, and what a wonderful natural jump he had.

Bella meanwhile descended gradually into adored lunacy: hunting, particularly jumping, fazed her, she was destined for a hack and pet. I could never think of parting with her brother's sister: no more than I could think of parting with the daughter of her dam.

The season ended with my first hunt on Dartmoor, which was to exert a similar pull to that of Exmoor and the Borders, its wild open spaces tempting me back again and again, and, a couple of times, all but getting me into trouble.

The Two Bridges Hunt Club is an annual, end-of-season joint meet of the four hunts whose territories divide the moor between them like the cross on an Easter bun. It was founded in 1929, in honour of the then Prince of Wales's annual hunting visits to his duchy. There is a dinner in it too. I'm not very good at dinners on my own, tend to dodge them, but I enjoyed this one.

We met next day an hour late, out of compliment to sore heads, at the East Dart Hotel, at Postbridge, which was to become my base for future Dartmoor expeditions. Of the hunting, I wrote "The whole thing was enormous fun and I wouldn't have missed a minute of it, even though it rained, sort of, all day, but I was not sorry when at last that long happy-sad horn note came. The end of the day; the end of my season – we hacked back to Foxworthy, where both Harry and I were stabled...."

1998 - 2001 – THINGS FALL APART...
B&SV – South Dorset – Wilton – Old Berks – New Forest
Exmoor – South Devon/Rallye Armor

FREELANCE journalism is a dodgy calling, that of a hunting correspondent doubly so, both are likely to end in tears, if not in hospital. After sundry misadventures on my young horses, including breaking a collar-bone off Dandy, and later having a fright with him in a bog on Darmoor, it began to dawn on me that their youth and my age were a foolish mix.

Also I was finding myself being quietly dropped by *Horse & Hound*, commissions were becoming rare; and then came the nightmare of Foot and Mouth Disease and a temporary stop to all hunting. I decided that when hunting re-started I would not...

...AND COME TOGETHER AGAIN – 2001 - 2003

Quantock Staghounds – Crow Hawking on Dartmoor
Four Hunts Meet on Exmoor – Marlborough College Beagles
Border – South Dorset – Axe Vale

.... when suddenly, out of a grey sky, came a shaft of light, and then another. The Editor of *The Field* asked me if I would stand in for their regular man, a serving soldier, who was required in Afghanistan, and the editorship of *Horse & Hound* changed hands. I was in business once more, and in joint harness yet again, with, as it was to turn out, some of my happiest days and best rides yet ahead of me.

If you have been so patient as to come with me thus far you must be wondering how and when this long, precarious tale will end. Let me just take you on my last visit to the Border Hunt, mention a happy day on a pinto with the Axe Vale, make a plea for staghunting, and then, I promise, we will skip lightly through to the *dénouement*, on Dartmoor.

THE BORDER HUNT

IT WAS not long, you may be sure, before I was asking the Editor of *The Field* if I might not have a day with Michael Hedley's Border hounds: he was not slow to agree. The wretched rump of urban ideologues that now rule Scotland had recently banned the sport. It seemed a good moment to see how hunts were coping - one third of the Border Hunt's territory is in Scotland.

The opening meet, at Rowhope Dipper, a sheep-wash in the Upper Coquet Valley in north Northumberland, was less than three miles south of the Border ridge of the Cheviots. Would a fox run that way? I found myself half-hoping so.

We had driven across Otterburn Ranges in thick mist, my host and old friend from army days, the Hunt Secretary, and I, drawing behind us the precious mare, which I shall call 'F', that he was generously lending me. Our route took us through Harbottle, where King William I plugged the valleys converging from the north at that spot with a strategically placed castle, and where Margaret Douglas, granddaughter of Henry VII, was born on 8 October 1515, during her mother's flight to England in more turbulent times. You walk with history, usually bloody history, in the Borders.

As we turned north up the River Coquet the mist lifted fitfully. By the time we had parked on the haugh, the flat lawn-like bottom of the valley, where sheep used to be folded for dipping, Windy Gyle, dominating the crest of the Cheviots and the Border, had come into view. Soon vehicles were arriving from north and south. Michael was there with his hounds, and his 90-year-old father and Joint Master, Ian – this was their jubilee year, the Hedley's had taken on the hounds from the Dodd and Robson dynasties in 1952.

The meet was a long one, an important ceremony, not to be hurried. As well as being a highly efficient fox-killing service – Michael and his hounds account for around 200 foxes every season - the local hunt is the main source of social contact and communication among the isolated shepherds and hill farmers across a huge area of upland Britain.

AS WE moved off, I heard Michael calling to his hounds. He has a wonderful, wild, ringing voice, much as, I would guess, Parson Jack Russell was famed for. The pack, many of which had been ranging at will in the dead bracken high above the meet on the steep side of Barrow Law, came to his call. He put them into nearby cover. Straightway they killed one fox: within minutes we were on the line of another.

If only foxhunting were that simple I could give you my own account of the hunt that followed. But a small band of us decided to climb an adjacent hill to get a better view of proceedings. Impenetrable mist descended, and we were blind and lost for the best part of an hour. Like Pooh and Piglet we repeatedly circled the slightly scary top of the aptly named Dumb Hope hill, multiplying our hoofprints as we sought to hit off the right track down.

Eventually, a single hound, vociferously hunting its own private line, gave us some sense of direction, the mist suddenly lifted, we found the rest of the pack and the field, and Michael brought me up-to-date. Hounds were still on the same fox, a game one, they had run a number of arabesques through places the names of which would mean as little to you as the did to me, and were hunting well.

It was a study to watch how relaxed Michael was, letting his hounds get on with their work with minimum interference. I barely heard the horn, and never a whip or a rate all day – yet I felt that there was total mutual awareness of what was wanted between hounds and huntsman. He was there to help and direct when needed, never to fuss.

Mostly the hounds just hunted on their own; now well together, now casting themselves wide; now silent, now speaking. Fifty-two hounds were out – the Border counts its fell hounds singly, as it does the foxes it catches. ("We use braces to hold up our trousers" Michel once told me). It was big pack, mostly light-coloured hounds, with a fine voice, a grand sight and sound.

SUDDENLY, briefly, the weather relented, and the beautiful panorama of the Borders sprang into view. Such space, such grandeur, as we southerners can only dream of. My pilot for the day said later, as we hacked home, "I really believe we have the best hunting country in all Britain". I could not disagree.

It is virtually untrammelled by roads, except those bequeathed by the Romans and by cattle drovers, with here and there the relics of ancient shepherding practices, such as circular stone stells. These sheep-shelters are scattered about the landscape as though the giants that made the landscape had been interrupted in a game of quoits. It is a timeless scene, with little if anything to annoy the eye, and everything to please it. Do you wonder that over the years I returned as often as I could?

The hunt continued, much as before, and over much the same ground. Hounds were always in view now, and we galloped as great deal. Willy Poole has described the Border as "one of the fastest packs of hounds I have ever seen. When they really run you need nerves of steel to keep in contention". Metal fatigue was indeed beginning to set in when the game fox was at last put to ground, by Dumb Hope Burn, dispatched, and Michael blew for home.

MY MOUNT, an Irish Draught/Thoroughbred cross, the best cross to get a hunter that I know, had been bred in Berwickshire. She gave me a great ride, took me hither and thither about the hillside on a loose rein much as seemed best to her. She was sure-footed, with a thorough understanding of the business in hand, our only disagreements had been over the question of mph.

I do like a horse that wants to go, and that knows its mind, so her method of carrying on suited me admirably. She was certainly full of beans, but I can only guess what she had done to deserve the name Fartina. She was evidently something of a favourite with members of the

Border field, but it was touch disconcerting, when we frequently erupted full tilt amongst them, to be greeted, albeit affectionately, with the words "Ah! Here comes old Farty".

As my pilot and I hacked back up the valley towards the Dipper, a commotion behind us told of someone down on the road, and a loose horse scarpering. Luckily, I had not yet slackened off my girth, so Fartina and I had one final gallop to unite the unfortunate rider with her mount. It was the sort of knight-errantry that sends a chap home from the hunting field with a really good opinion of himself, the icing on the cake.

APART from the kindness of my hosts, two things have drawn me back to hunt with the Border hounds as often as various editors would allow. One is the breathtaking beauty of the country, and sense of total freedom and remoteness from all things Blairish. But also I have been drawn by the wish to see, and especially to hear, Michael Hedley hunt his hounds.

His son Peter runs the family farm at Overacres, his wife Carole, a great support, teaches the infants at Otterburn School, and Michael, single-handed, runs the kennel. Small wonder the hounds know him; small wonder an invisible thread seems to stretch between them on the broad hillside.

Trueman, an old broken-coated hound of his was living out a restful retirement at Low Leam, close by where I was staying. Ocasionally, anxious reports would circulate of a "dead dog" lying in the Bellingham road. No such thing. It was Trueman taking his siesta – he was not as active in these latter times as he had used to be.

But when hounds had met there, in the week before my visit, the old boy struggled to his feet, lumbered across, and, placing a great foot firmly on each of Michael's shoulders, greeted his old huntsman. He insisted on rejoining the pack that day: lapped by a ringing fox, he briefly led the chase.

PIKEY

"DON'T forget your waterwings!" a kind neighbour had prompted when he heard that I was visiting the Axe Vale, whose hounds had recently been photographed swimming across the swollen River Axe.

I needn't have worried. Although we were to ford the Coly, the Axe was no more than an occasional distant view, snaking its way to the sea at Seaton. And, far from being in for a drowning, I was in luck. The Harriers had a busy, sunny, foxy day ending with an evening hunt that produced the run of the season.

The meet was at Master-cum-huntsman Roy Williams's farm, and my day began as it was to end in his wife's hospitable kitchen along with the terriermen, earth-stoppers, Uncle Tom Cobbleigh and all…. and I learnt about Pikey.

If there is one thing I like it is a coloured horse. They seem to have hybrid qualities, I have never known a bad one, but they have one drawback for someone in my line of business – I call it sore thumb syndrome. Everybody knows exactly who and where you are and how you are managing, or not, to get about their country.

Pikey, such a deliciously incorrect name, could get one jailed for using it no doubt, turned out to be tricolour, ie a skewbald with, in his case, here and there, little bits of black. Sixteen hands, six years old, with a pony face and soup-plate feet, he was Cornish bred, with Cruise Missile somewhere in his ancestry, an eventing mother and a van horse for his dad. Just the ticket: my gypsy friend and I were soon to become blood brothers.

I don't remember ever riding a borrowed horse that suited me so well; what is more Pikey left me without a single ache after more than six hours in the saddle.

ROY had out 18 couple of his mostly pale coloured West Country Harriers. People often, quite naturally, think that the term harrier has something to do with hares, but it is not so. They are called harriers because of the way they used to hunt, like the bird of that name. Historically harriers were bred to hunt roe deer, fox or hare. Only in comparatively recent times did they become solely hare hounds.

The Axe Vale, like many packs of modern Harriers, changed to hunting foxes some years back, but they still wear the green coat, and are proud of their distinctive title. Their hounds, although now bred a bit bigger than some hare-hunting harriers, are all entered in the Harrier Stud Book.

After moving off we found right away – we were barely to draw blank all day – in a steep bank of bracken and gorse close by the meet. "A sure find, but difficult to get away from" one member of the field commented, and so it was to prove.

We spent an enjoyable hour up and down and around about that place. The sun was shining, it felt more like June than January, and we were on old turf – such a luxury if you live in a deep clay vale. And the music of the hounds, especially when it echoed up from the bottom of the goyle, was a feast for the ears.

We were following an inventive Field Master. An old hunter trial course was handy, and somehow he managed to weave a fair amount of jumping into our perambulations. Very early in proceedings that first, worrying jump was behind us – a drop over some stout timber – Pikey accelerated, and did a bright confident arching rainbow over it. Such joy, evidently I could forget about that side of things and just let him get on with it.

∾

THE first hunt ended inconclusively. A second fox, found in one of Roy's own hedges, was soon put to ground, and the next, of which we had a good view, took us into what the map gives the German-sounding name of Morganhayes, but which the locals call Morning Covert – "You get there in the morning and stay there all day" someone muttered.

In fact we had a lot of fun there. I attached myself to Roy, and it was a joy to watch him, and to listen to him, with his hounds. Morganhayes is a big hanging, steep wood, of 200 acres or so, and there was more than one fox afoot. Roy got one away, but, as luck would have it, on to land where we were not welcome. Hounds had to be called off, and we hacked down to and forded the swollen River Coly.

We drew on, found, hunted – hounds busy all the time – put one to ground, but otherwise nothing coming to much. The sun was starting to give notice, but I heard Roy say "I'm not stopping yet".

I admire most huntsmen, but I admire best those who, carrying the responsibility of it all, yet manage to be pleasant, and to make even the humblest the members of the field feel they are a welcome part of what is going on.

Roy was just such a one, the most genial of huntsmen, with a kind word for everyone. I was told that once, when a child on a bolting pony cut in front of him in a gateway, all he said was "I wish my horse could go that fast".

∾

IT WAS past 4pm when hounds found in Downhayne Brake, a triangular patch of big fir trees, up above the hunt kennels.

It was one of those scenes that stick in the mind. There weren't many of us still out. Hounds spoke, and the sun, which had not failed us all day, was shooting low beams in defilade, through the ranks of tree trunks.

What followed turned out to be an amazing hound hunt, lasting the best part of an hour, hounds mostly in view, either below us running the river bank, or above us in a wooded crest.

The hunt finally petered out, as hunts sometimes will. At the finish, as light was failing, very few of us were left, and the pack split, some, from their muzzles, had evidently marked to ground. We began the long business of getting the pack together.

At last I said "Good night and thank you" to my pinto friend, and let off his girth. Like all the horses still out, he had done about as much as you could expect of one horse on a day that really needed two. He had given me a ride to remember.

The Terrierman gave me a lift, as we drove at hound pace, the tired pack in our headlights, along with the hunt establishment and sundry other faithful helpers, such as all hunts have, and who pop up when they are needed. Roy every now and again blowing, all the way home to the kennels... and to that warm hospitable kitchen where the day had started.

LUCY AGAIN

ONCE UPON a time I used to be a bit queasy about staghunting. I was uneasy at the discomforting of that noble beast, which is, after all, not vermin like a fox. That was before I got close to the sport, and to the people whose lives are centred on it. Then I came to understand that no one does more for, cares more for, or knows more about, that no one in the truest sense of the word more respects, Exmoor's precious herd of wild red deer than the farmers who tolerate its depredations on their land, and the harbourers, the huntsmen, and the regular followers of the three stag hunts on Exmoor and the Quantocks.

Whenever I have written about it I have consciously addressed myself to those who, as I once was, might be ambivalent about staghunting. This was very much in my mind when I wrote this piece for *The Field* in 2002, I was pleading for a cause, the virtue of which I had come very strongly to believe in. It describes a day with the Quantock Stag Hounds (QSH) in March of that year, the very day on which MPs in London SW1 were debating the future of what they choose to call "hunting with dogs".

THE meet, at Crowcombe Park Gate, would have been a puzzling occasion for even the most be-medalled veteran Westminster class warrior. Neither a toff nor a top hat was to be seen, never a cut-glass accent to be heard, nor indeed a sight of an 'anti', the QSH not being much troubled by that sort. There was just the usual large gathering of Quantock people, including of course Richard Down, whose whole life has been devoted to and bound up with staghunting, with 20½ couple of his bitch hounds.

The QSH only hunts with bitches, which are so much more biddable than dog hounds, and better suited to their restricted country. I was glad to see an all black hound of engaging character called Chequebook amongst them. "She never misses a day", one of the Masters reassuringly told me.

I had witnessed Chequebook's debut, a deer-addict drafted in from a neighbouring pack of foxhounds several seasons before. Smaller than any of her colleagues, she was an easy hound for the visitor to spot, and she always seemed particularly attentive to the Huntsman, particularly anxious to please.

It was no surprise to see Chequebook drawn by Richard among the tufters, the especially trusted hounds, seven-and-a-half couple of them, he was to use for the difficult work of singling out from the herd the stag that had been selected overnight by the harbourer to be hunted.

The rest of the pack, loudly clamouring and complaining, were bundled back into the hound van after the formalities of the meet to wait until they should be sent for. And off we jogged, northward a mile, to Somerton Combe.

IT HAS been well said that " a big horse on short legs is one that will see the end of more runs with the QSH": but, for my taste, if you admit comfort to the equation, a sure-footed, sensible thoroughbred takes a lot of beating. I was however on Lucy, who is tall, lissom, and near clean-bred . She was an old and valued friend, lent me by another such, my occasional Dorset neighbour, the Vicomte Hugh le Hardÿ de Beaulieu.

Hounds were soon speaking, below us in Slaughterhouse Combe, announcing the phase of staghunting that really tests the huntsman's skill and patience. Both were to be tested to the full. With great difficulty, and after about an hour, Richard got his tufters away on a single stag, when word came that an injured hind had been spotted on the hill.

Hounds were immediately called off the hunted stag, and, for a further hour they tracked the poor maimed creature until the huntsman could safely shoot it. It was a road or poaching casualty no doubt, saved from a lingering death by the intervention of the hunt. My mind did not often stray to Westminster that day, but it was impossible not to wish that some of those self-righteous, wilfully ignorant MPs could have witnessed what the QSH were doing, whilst they were preparing to debate a subject so many of them know and care so little bout.

It was well into the afternoon before Richard could resume the proper business of the day. For some time the main body of the pack had been making their presence felt off-stage, parked in the van behind us, above Halsway Zoggs. He picked them up and went to look for a fresh stag. This would be a difficult undertaking with the full pack, but the tufters had done enough, and needed reinforcements.

I COULD tell you, if I thought you would be interested, exactly what happened in the following two hours, not because I 'read' the hunt, that is difficult enough for an habitué of staghunting, but because I went through it all afterwards, as one does, with those who know. A rather dejected Richard Down told me that evening that "it all went 'pear-shaped'". A proud man, immensely keen to show off his hounds, and show sport, he had had to give up the day's promise in order to dispatch the injured hind, and had had to take his hounds home at four o'clock.

Suffice it to say that we were kept very busy, saw countless deer, briefly hunted some of them, scampered hither and thither very enjoyably. The going, except where the heather had been burnt, was completely blind, but sure-footed Lucy blithely jumped the gorse, porpoise-like, to dodge the prickles. Up there in the Quantocks you go back a week or so in the season: there was not much sign of spring, all were sombre winter colours, relieved just by emerald moss and cuprous lichen, with a great deal of water lying everywhere.

We had terrific views out over the Bristol Channel to Lundy and to Wales. A gale had blown all day, and it had rained a bit, but not to notice. Nelson, an old stable-mate of Lucy's, kept heaving-to alongside. Three times I saw his rider replace the same cigarette, unlit, in its packet before she finally got it going when we for once descended into the lee of the oak scrub in Holford Combe.

It had been a memorable, wild, tiring, useful, happy day, and it was not until past 10 o'clock that evening that we heard the news of the House of Commons vote – 364 to 174 for a total ban. I was put in mind of something the late Bill Leyland, then Chairman of the QSH, had said to me of staghunting's opponents some years before. "These people, however well-meaning, intelligent and book-learned, do not understand what makes the countryside tick. They would attack the whole social fabric and balance of this community, and have not a clue what damage they are bent on".

2004/2005- THE CRUNCH
South Dorset – Park Beagles – RA Salisbury Plain – Dartmoor
February 19th – South Dorset Protest Meet.

ALL OUR seasons since 1997 had of course been overshadowed by the threat to hunting, and interwoven with marches, and with unwelcome, uncongenial political activity. Now came the final season of hunting untrammelled by oppressive, farcical law. Along with everyone else, I was determined to make the very most of it, and had a full programme of visits planned, however, my luck failed to hold.

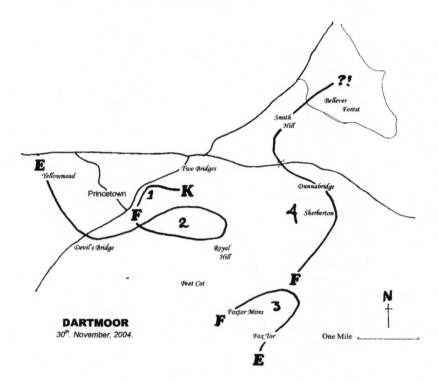

DARTMOOR
30ᵗʰ. November, 2004.

FOLLOWING the Dartmoor Hunt lorry from the kennels to the meet, I became aware of a pair of eyes watching me intently through a small grill in the tailgate. This I was later to learn was Tuneful, there was no mistaking her face, and I had plenty of time to study it. A great deal of nose-wrestling went on, other hounds no doubt wanting to take a peep at me, but Tuneful mostly seemed to hold her own.

It's lucky we don't know how the day will end when we set off hunting. Tuneful got hit by a car on a road, and ended her day on wheels, though no serious harm done: I was to find myself, darkness falling, unpaid, unofficial and totally useless whipper-in, alone with the Huntsman, trying to help round up Tuneful's companions at the end of a long and exciting day when all bar two couple of the pack got lost.

I had stayed the night nearby at Marldon, and it had seemed a good plan to start the day at the kennels, to see again that busy scene, a hunt getting on the road. Very impressive it had been too. Just 3½ people run the Dartmoor Hunt kennels, over thirty couple of hounds, and eleven horses, which Huntsman and Master Michael Weir, who was a farrier before he was a huntsman, himself shoes. It was the tidiest yard I have ever seen, and not a voice was raised, except that of the hounds, as each member of the team went quietly about their business. "We'll be off in two minutes", Mike said to me, and so we were.

Dartmoor is an awesome place to the occasional visitor, never losing its theatrical effect at first sight. Soon its savage skyline came into view, we were tracking its steep twisting narrow roads, threading its hump-backed bridges… and Tuneful was ogling me. "Unfenced road!" a sign warned – "Good" I thought; then "Animals on the road!" – "Better", and Princetown, with its grim prison (so handy for our loving rulers to utilise in coming months?) was ahead of us. We had arrived.

I was introduced to Claire, the Whipper-in… and to Rocky, my mount for the day, a seven-year-old thoroughbred by Rock Hopper. That sounded promising breeding for Dartmoor, although he had been bought at Ascot sales. I was to have an adventurous time on Rocky, until we got to understand each other, more than once I thought we might be parting company and there might truly be a 'horror show'. As the attachments on his saddle showed, he was used to carrying the horn – I don't think he thought much to carrying the pencil – he wanted to be right up with hounds. He was I think my most challenging mount in fifteen years, but, once we had settled, he proved to be a brilliant and enjoyable ride.

AFTER the meet in the Plume of Feathers yard, hounds soon found a fox, hunted him across the nearby filter beds, and caught him in Oakery. Then, to quote our Huntsman "Found in the filter beds again, he went up over the end of Royal Hill, through Bachelor's Hall, through South Hessary Covert, to the gardens at Princetown, ran along the outside of the gardens, crossed the main Yelverton-Princetown road out into the Spooners' country at Devil's elbow (where poor Tuneful bought it) and they put him to ground in the rubble pile at Yellowmeade".

This was a breathtaking circular gallop. If you so much as touched the brakes you lost the hunt, yet the going underfoot was the stuff nightmares are made of. Rocks everywhere, traps galore, thanks to some brilliant environmental wheeze whereby the farmers are not allowed to winter-graze their stock on the moor, overgrown quiffs of grass concealing every-thing. You just had to follow a good pilot, and trust your horse.

As we hacked back into Dartmoor country I fell to thinking about what makes hunting on the Moor so special – so different from what most of us who hunt know and enjoy. Apart from the obvious, the wild beauty of the country – at that particular moment the sun, already dropping, had turned the distant surface of Plymouth Sound to silver – I think that the infor-mality of it, and the intimacy with hounds is the key. Where else can you ride right up behind the huntsman (so long as you have the wit to hold your tongue) without being rebuked, hear him thinking aloud as he lets his hounds get on with hunting, feel that you are really part of what is going on, not just an also-ran?

"That's something like it; another hunt like that this afternoon, and we shall feel we have had a good day" the Field Master said to me as we hacked on to the next draw. "We drew South Plantation and Peat Cot blank", continuing the Huntsman's narrative, "to Foxtor Mires, where we found and had a circular hunt that eventually ended with the fox going to ground in Foxtor Girt".

"Then we drew back to the big bog under Royal Hill, found a fox there, ran to Little Sherberton, back to Dunnabridge Covert, crossed the main road at the Cherry Brook, crossed Muddy Lake, Smith Hill, and (as we later discovered) into Bellever Forest".

IT WAS sometime in that fourth hunt of a busy day, by my reckoning when the field was looking down onto where the Cherry Brook joins the West Dart, that hounds got clean away from us. And so it was that, in failing light, we ended up on the Ashburton road, the wrong side of Two Bridges, with just two couple of hounds, and as many opinions as to which direction the pack had taken as there were remaining members of the field.

"Nice hunt, pity about the hounds" a jokey foot-follower said, but it wasn't really a laughing matter – virtually the whole pack was lost in that vast wilderness. "I'm convinced they crossed over" Mike said leading the small band of us across the moor up north towards the Widecombe road.

He was right: as the man hunting hounds generally is. Word came that they were in Bellever, a great tract of forestry all but surrounding a tor of that name. It was "Good night!" to the faithful few, and off we jogged into the gloom, leaving the meet further and further behind us (how and when was I ever going to get home?). There was just the Huntsman and his Whipper-in, plus Madam, Glucose, Traveller, Pidgeon and me.

Soon we were in the depth of the forestry, Mike for ever blowing, Claire's melodious voice echoing as she ranged wide in the various drifts and tracks. Hounds returned in dribs and drabs, until, after the best part of an hour, we had very nearly the whole pack together again. And that is how it came about that my fifteen years of writing about hunting both began and ended in a dreamlike situation: alone with a huntsman and his hounds.

LIKE Tuneful on the way to her day's hunting from the Plume of Feathers, I was happily unaware of what Fate had waiting round the corner. Just eight days after what was perhaps my most challenging ride as a mounted scribbler I found myself pinned to the ground under half a ton of horse.

Dandy had put both of his front feet in a rabbit hole, done a cartwheel, and ended up with his back-end facing the way we had been travelling, with my legs trapped underneath him, fortunately clear of the saddle – he was 'cast' and winded, neither of us was able to move.

We had been cantering up the edge of a meadow. This was lucky for me as I was thrown onto the foot of a hedge-bank, which prevented Dandy from rolling completely over. As it was, his two hind hooves were pointing skywards, rather pathetically, just a foot or eighteen inches from my face.

My first thought, since he lay completely still, was that he had broken his back. I grabbed one of his hooves, shook it, and said "Come on Dandikins, wake up!" Fortunately he paid no attention, for when he did come to, some five minutes later, his struggles to get up were extremely violent. By then my companion had had the presence of mind to drag me clear, before going off to seek help.

It seemed rather a long time before she returned. Dandy in due course struggled to his feet, went off and grazed unconcernedly – he was totally unhurt – I found, when I got up that I was rooted to the ground, couldn't lift either foot to take a single pace, so lay down again and listened to the bells of Sydling St Nicholas church in the valley below. It was a Sunday morning, early December: I wasn't very comfortable and was getting rather cold.

In due course came the sound of a Landrover, then a helicopter – you can guess the rest. The Air Ambulance crew were superb, just like the crew of a tank in a good regiment, knew exactly what they were up to, and were full of self-confidence, verve and humour.

SO ended of my plans for a full hunting season in 2004/2005; but my great aim, when I got home from hospital, was to be back in the saddle in time to sit out the meet on 19 February at which hunts all over the country registered their contempt for Parliament's hunting ban. This we managed, thanks to Diana having heroically kept Dandy in work for me over a very difficult Christmas.

What comes next? We go on hunting, to the limit of what is permitted by a farcical law, and, I suppose, I go on writing about it: I meant to stop last season, but this is no time to quit.

ENVOI

"GOOD morning Master!" I said to the young man, barely half my age, leading his hounds down Park Lane. "Good morning Brigadier!" he replied with a generous sweep of his hat; and "Good morning Tim!" to his Kennel Huntsman, "Good morning Sir!" came the smiling answer. How I love these old formalities, they mean a great deal, and nothing, yet connect with so much that I care about.

It was the last day of August, we were just twenty-four hours back from Italy, when Rory had, so courteously, rung to say that he was bringing his hounds this way next morning (to hunt legally of course), meeting at 6am. Goodness knows how long he and Tim had been out of their beds when I met them – barely unpacked, and with this book due in Tiverton, there was no way that I could get out hunting properly, but I was determined just to take a look at hounds.

I was on my feet in the lane when they passed, Bella's rein looped over my arm, a large plastic lemonade bottle in one hand, the other holding a fistful of fag-packets and sweet wrappers. Park Lane had missed my regular attentions whilst we had been away.

There was so much in that meeting, a good moment to drop dead really. The pack that I have followed on and off for over sixty years, just the three of us with our horses – I could see some of the usual faithful foot-followers further up the road.

It was a gamble bringing Bella, she usually lights up rather alarmingly when I take her near hounds, but it was her turn, I'd got Dandy's back down the day before. "That's asking for trouble" Diana had said to me about something else some days before, "I like asking for trouble every now and then" I had replied, "I know you do…".

It seems to me that it is our birthright to live a little near the edge: elbowroom is everything. I leave you, in that favourite Dorset lane on the slope of Dungeon Hill, with a hunting man's farewell. "Good night!".

APPENDIX

EXPLORING THE OLD SHERBORNE ROAD
(Friday, 15 July, 2005)

WE ARE standing, as many of you will not need telling, in an old droveway... a very old droveway. It was the route by which, until the railways came, and refrigerators were invented, cattle, sheep, pigs, poultry even were driven up at the back end of the summer, in easy stages so as not to lose condition, from farms and grasslands in the west to markets nearer the centres of population, for sale, slaughter and salting down for the winter.

This is Boys Hill Drove. If when you get home you lay a ruler on the map you will see that it connects with similar bits of surviving droveway west and east from here; Holwell Drove being the nearest and perhaps the best example. Where they were headed we cannot be sure, whether it was just to Sturminster, to Salisbury, or on to Smithfield in London we can only guess now, because droving has left very little written history.

But droving's history is indelibly written on this part of Dorset. Here you can see the full width of the droveway – well hedged you may be sure – what farmer would want somebody else's cattle getting into his precious grass? And well watered too – out of sight now, but you just crossed it coming here, is a tributary of the Caundle Brook.

Where the bridge is today would then have been a much-trampled muddy ford. You can picture the thirsty beefs quickening their pace, perhaps hear them bellowing, as they sensed the presence of the water after a long day's walk, and came winding over the crest here.

You can imagine the drovers also, and their dogs – lurchers probably, dual-purpose, herding the beasts by day, and poaching for the pot at night. Drovers were no doubt tough, hard men – this was our Wild West, they were our cowboys. But they would have been trustworthy, respected for their skill, and they had many farming families' fortunes in their care.

YOU COULD be forgiven for thinking that you are standing at a T-junction here on this spot (GR 665102), but you are not – you are standing at an old crossroads, once no doubt a quite important one. For, centuries ago, before stage-coaches made some sort of smooth road surface necessary, and before the arrival of the motorcar made tarmac essential, the traveller heading for Dorchester from Sherborne had a choice of at least two roads, the present A 352 that we all use today, or the Old Sherborne Road. We are standing at the place where that old road crossed the equally ancient drove.

This is what Ronald Good, writing in 1940, says about it in his book *The Old Roads of Dorset*. "The Old Sherborne Road is no longer a through route... it ends abruptly at a T-junction, opposite which is a wide field gate, but there is now no trace of a continuation through it. However, nearly all this part of the Vale was largely open country not so long ago, and the medieval road must have run on over this to near, or past Osehill Green, probably to the inn at Middlemarsh".

Well, I don't often find myself in disagreement with the Reverend Ronald Good and his wonderful, very precious and rare book, but I can't agree with him when he says that there is no trace of the old road beyond this point – if you know what to look for there are plenty of traces of this, as I call it, Ghost Road. And we are going to try and look for them now, to rediscover a lost fragment of the Old Sherborne Road, from one long forgotten crossroads to another.

AS IN detective stories, you look for clues, and the first clue is to be found by looking back the way the road has come, north, up Broke Lane as it is called. This was little more than a farm track when I first knew it, if you drove a car up it you had to do so with great care, Wizard Bridge, about a mile up, had a hump in it that you could belly a car on if you forgot to take it at an angle, as I did more than once in my mother's old Morris 8, when I was learning to drive.

But if Broke Lane was rough, it was straight, dead straight, it knew exactly where it was going, and where it had come from. And this is the first point to remember when you are trying to trace old roads... the people who used them were not tourists or trippers out for a pretty walk, they were intent on getting from A to B by the shortest convenient route. You might not think so, looking at some of our wiggly roads today, but you may be sure that, like the Romans, people went as straight across the country as the various obstacles in their way allowed.

The line of Broke Lane runs like an arrow back to Sherborne, hitting the town more or less where the level crossing is today. It is significant that, before it finally drops down Gainsborough Hill to the town, it passes a place called Gallows Plot. Gallows were erected where travellers could not miss them – from were they were sure to carry home with them the grim message of the gibbet. This suggests very strongly to me that the Old Sherborne Road was in fact, in its day, more important and more frequently used than what is now the A 352.

And, again, if you put a ruler on Broke Lane in the direction we are going, you will find that its line runs equally straight to what is now the Hunter's Moon, the old White Horse, at Middlemarsh. As we search for traces of this Ghost Road we are going to follow our noses as straight as the country allows.

But before we go any further I want to thank Brian Batten for very generously allowing us to leave the public way here and cross his land.

IF THE first clue is the line and direction of the road, the beeline from 'A to B', the second is to be found in the features of the landscape. If there were footpaths, bridleways or ancient parish boundaries, they would tell us something, but there aren't any here. Next to look for are the shapes of fields and woods, and the line of hedges.

Ronald Good tells us that the land was open not so long ago; he was looking back at least a century and a half from today. I think we may take it that our road was established long before these hedges were planted – but what is almost equally certain is that this long straight hedge, when it was planted, took account of the line of the then existing road.

Look at this hedge, look at the shape of this field. Its name is Long Common, that tells a story. Brian tells me that when his father first took on the land Long Common was rough land, all over gorse; we can be quite certain that it was not all that long ago a neglected strip of common land that carried the old road.

Look how this wood has been sited – its very name is a giveaway, Davis's Plantation, it's not an ancient wood but one planted by a Mr Davis. Hedge wood and field all leave us in no doubt that the old road ran down the middle of the field here.

Before we follow it however just one caution. It is all too easy, when you use the word 'road', to picture in your mind a neat modern road, tarmac running between two verges. Old roads weren't like that, especially country roads, they would have wandered this way and that, perhaps taking up the whole width of the field, as different stretches became boggy and impassable, or were occasionally repaired. They were horrible, dirty places to travel, deep and dangerous in winter, dusty as hell in summer.

So if you are trying to picture the old road running down this long narrow field, think of it as a whole lot of tracks weaving along and criss-crossing each other like a very old frayed rope. And if you want to imagine the travellers on it, think of people on foot, on horseback, or maybe in charge of strings of pack-horses carrying goods. Vehicles, probably some sort of rough horse-drawn cart, would be the exception rather than the rule.

All, you may sure, if they were going in the same direction we are, would have been longing to get home to Osehill Green, Glanvilles Wootton, Loaders Farm, the Inn at Middlemarsh, or distant Dorchester. Travelling in those days was a struggle. Let us also get on our way....

HERE the detective is in luck, there are two very strong clues. Who can doubt that where we are standing now, in what I call the Berkeley gap – this is Berkeley's Plantation on our right – is an actual stretch of the old road? It is more than a clue, it's a confession! Look at this ash tree, it's a pollard, and because of that probably a lot older than at first sight you might think.

Pollards were visited by the woodman with his axe and saw every few years to provide fence timber, before barbed wire was invented, and for firewood. But because pollards stuck out like sore thumbs, looked a bit like skinheads when the woodman had recently visited them, they were also widely used as boundary and way-markers. Perhaps this old ash tree served such a dual purpose.

And here's the other clue, look at the position of 'The Orchard', as that house is called. If houses were built other than facing or backing south you may be sure that they were built facing onto a road. 'The Orchard' tells us as clear as if it could speak that the Old Sherborne Road ran in front of or behind it; in fact I believe that it followed what is now the house's long narrow garden and driveway.

I am not quite sure exactly how it crossed the B 3146, the familiar road to Glanvilles Wootton, onto Robin and Paul Goodfellow's land, whether or not it touched Osehill Farm here, as an air photograph lent me by Richard Clarke suggests. But as it winds gently over the only hill on our short journey, Loader's Hill, there are another couple of splendid clues. First, you can actually see etched on the ground, at least I fancy I can, the line of the old trackway as it winds round the crest of the hill.

Secondly, there are those old oak trees standing beside the track. One is an old pollard, see its truncated shape, how its branches grow out from where the trunk was first cut through two centuries or more, probably

The Clues

Broke Lane

Davis's Plantation
&
Long Common

Berkeley's Plantation
& 'Berkeley's Gap'

'The Orchard'

Old Oaks in Hebditches

Loader's Farm (ruin)

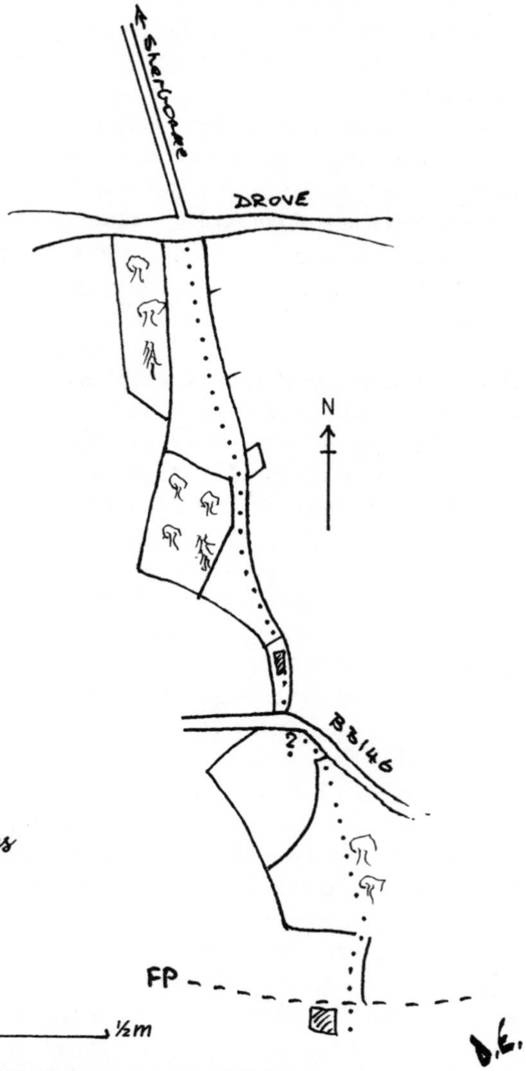

Scale: └─────────────┘ ½ m

A SHERBORNE

DROVE

N ↑

B3146

FP

D.E.

A LOST FRAGMENT OF THE OLD SHERBORNE ROAD

much more, ago. I feel sure that that old tree told the traveller "This is your route onward, over the hill to Loader's Farm".

SO HERE we are at Loader's Farm, once a busy outlying settlement of Glanvilles Wootton, now long deserted. Many of us came here on an earlier Village Outing: some of us can remember Ned Crew, our old village postman, the last survivor to live amongst us who was actually born here.

How the road went on from here to the inn at Middlemarsh I don't know. It will have gone as straight as possible you may be sure; but what exact route it followed is perhaps a puzzle for another day.

For the moment let us end, as we started, at what was once a cross-roads, where what is now just a footpath from our village, on its busy way westwards, crossed over the Old Sherborne Road.